SOUTH CAROLINA REVIEW

VOLUME 54.1, FALL 2021

FRIENDS OF *THE SCR*

The editorial board wishes to acknowledge the generous support of our patrons: Wayne K. Chapman and Janet M. Manson; John Idol, Jr.; Ronald Moran; and Dick and Doris Calhoun.

**CLEMSON®
UNIVERSITY
PRESS**

The South Carolina Review is published by Clemson University Press
801 Strode Tower, Clemson, SC 29634
© 2021 Clemson University   ISSN 0038-3163

Typeface: Minion Pro
Cover Art: *Big Pink Blanket*, 2021, Carolyn Kerecman

EDITORIAL CORRESPONDENCE
The Editor, *The South Carolina Review*
Center for Electronic and Digital Publishing
Clemson University, Strode Tower, Box 340522
Clemson, SC 29634-0522
Tel. (864) 656-3151 (864) 656-5399   Fax (864) 656-1345

SUBSCRIPTION INFORMATION*

Individual	*Institutional*
Single Copy $17	Single Copy $17
One-year subscription $28	One-year subscription $33
Two-year subscription $40	Two-year subscription $47
Three-year subscription $54	Three-year subscription $61

*Including postage and handling in the US only. Add an additional $10 per
annum for subscribers outside the United States and Canada.

Subscribe and order copies from our web site
http://www.clemson.edu/cedp/cudp/scr/scrintro.htm

The South Carolina Review is indexed in the *MLA International Bibliography*,
Humanities International Complete, *Index to Periodical Fiction*, and *Book
Review Index*. *SCR* belongs to the Council of Editors of Learned Journals
and the Council of Literary Magazines and Presses. Content from *SCR*
37.1 onward is also available vis ProQuest's online database (http://www.
proquest.com).

Entered as fourth-class mail at Clemson, SC 29634-0522

CONTENTS

Poem in Which a Bird is Never Mentioned

Or moon, or sky, or sun. It has no water. No path. No dusk or dawn. It is not a poem that speaks of stars. There is no deep of night. No smell of jasmine. No sound of insects whirring. No chirps no sighs or wails. There is no body. Nobody. Not an I or a you. Not a you that is an I, or an I that is a we. Or a we that is a me. This poem has no mother. No lover. No hurt to unbury and lay bare. This poem has no trees. No dirt or mud or grass. There is no field of poppies or snow. There is no field. No season. No nest and no egg. No wolf, no whale, no dream. Even a dream of nothing is not in this poem. No realization or epiphany. No resolution no yearning. There is no fruit, goddamnit. No garden and no prayer. This poem will not tell a story. It won't be avant-garde. It won't play with language. There is no music. No song. This poem has no storm or blistering heat. No swimsuit no scarf no undies. No childhood furniture. No injury. No god, no ghost.

Photo by Ben Katarzynski

Even Days

The bitches who knew Lina since kindergarten send their minivan moms to mourn in their place. With their frosted blonde highlights and expensive perfume, they cry over Lina, putting their cheeks against mine and leaving peach makeup behind. Motherfuckers who'd stopped talking to Lina by eleventh grade posted RIP on her wall, tagged her in photos, shared her obituary from the Syracuse *Post-Standard*. 21, *died Thursday at home.*

I exit the kitchen, that sauna of grief where, despite the central air, despite the fact that the food is catered and neither of the two ovens has been used, it feels steamy, like everyone's breath is trapped inside. Besides, I can't handle another conversation with a minivan mom, where they touch my face in pity before asking me about my career aspirations. They still know me as the scholarship kid.

More people would have come, but it's the week of college graduation. I, too, should be walking across the stage, receiving fancy parchment, taking photos in my Class of '09 T-shirt.

I'll miss the LSAT I scheduled, and I left all my shit at my roommate's family's house in Brooklyn, where I'm supposed to be living until I figure out what's next. My campus job in the library has ended. So here I am, suspended, with nothing on my calendar, following a cue out of my best friend's kitchen, while her body turns cold underground.

Emily has made the sign, her finger pinched to one of her nostrils, in the kitchen doorway, just in time. At least she showed up for the wake. She didn't come for the service or the burial at St. Mary's, where a steel machine lowered Lina's coffin deeper and deeper into the earth's hungry jaws. Where Juan finally broke down, sank to his knees, wailed at the earth, "How could you be so stupid?"

Emily and I sneak down into the basement, close ourselves into the bathroom. I remember the first time Lina caught us in here. That was before she tried snorting anything, when she was still freaked out by the idea of putting something up your nose. Plus, Lina had cousins in Mexico who'd died because Americans couldn't get enough. She didn't speak to either of us for days afterwards, and back then, days were their own little universes.

3

Emily has a whole kit: a bright orange Clinique makeup bag with a metal straw, razor, and little mirror inside.

She sniffs up her line quickly and holds the mirror up to my face. I see my own eyes magnified. My heart rate shoots up. I feel the pulse in my inner thigh. The bathroom feels stuffy. I turn on the switch for the fan, remember discovering it during my first time sleeping over at Lina's, one of the many luxuries I never thought about until I met people with money—a fan to blow the bad bathroom particles into undetectable smithereens.

Emily shuts it off. "Dude," she says, and I realize the circulation has blown her neat lines apart, whisking some particles onto the floor.

"Shit. I'm so sorry."

"Chill," Emily says. Any other time, she'd be pissed, but she's gentle now.

I think at any moment, Lina will be knocking on the door, getting mad at us for sneaking off. She will storm in, drunk, yelling about not wanting cokeheads in her house. But that was before she got into pills.

Emily and I are two of the few who know about the pills, we and Lina's parents. There were official stories told every time she went to rehab—they were her "artist residencies."

As soon as I enter the dense air of the kitchen, Patrick comes over and claps me on the shoulder. "I've been looking for you," he says. He pulls me toward the stairs. My heart is trampoline jumping, intestines clenching around emptiness.

He brings me up to Lina's room. Everything is the same as the last time I was here, right before we left for our first year of college, when she would take a medical leave the first semester to go to rehab. Bright yellow walls, dream catcher above her bed, Bob Marley posters.

Patrick points to a place on the carpet, next to the bed.

"That's where we found her," he says. When I look closely enough at the carpet, I see the stain there, not quite in the shape of a body, but some amorphous form.

"We tried CPR, but it was too late. There was a whole medium pizza from Mario and Salvo's. And an empty bottle of vodka."

"Oh my God," I say. I'd heard of kids dying from alcohol poisoning, those frat house hazing horror stories. I'd learned to turn my friends on their left sides in their dorm beds.

"We're still waiting on the autopsy report. I didn't find any needles, or pill bottles, but… you know Lina. If she wanted to hide something, she'd find a way."

He sighs deeply.

"You know, things were looking up for her," Patrick says. "She was enrolled in fall classes at OCC—Spanish, Psychology, Art History. I have a lot of suicidal patients. They don't make plans for the future."

"Right," I say, nodding vigorously, wiping cocaine snot from my face with the back of my hand.

Patrick tells me to come over to look at her jewelry box, picks out things he thinks I might like. A gold-plated bracelet, a silver Tiffany's necklace, her turquoise and silver ring.

He pulls out an empty drawer. "That's weird," he says.

Missing: the set she inherited from her late grandmother, Patrick's mother—a matching watch, earrings, ring, and bracelet, diamonds and emeralds set in platinum.

She'd been so sad when that grandmother died, she locked herself in her room with a handle of Bacardi and missed three days of school and showers. Patrick had called me to come over, and when the Chili's buffalo chicken salad I brought her couldn't get her out of bed, she let me in, and I came into her bed and we ate there together and watched *Gladiator* for the hundredth time. As always, it helped her to watch men tear each other apart.

"What do you think happened?" I don't bring up the two months last year when the boyfriend lived with them. Why would they let him stay here? Maybe they were afraid that if they didn't, Lina would disappear for days, and there would be no checking on her over the intercom, no family dinners over which they could study her pupils.

Someone is there in the parked car at the end of the driveway.

I see the driver, a white guy in a white muscle shirt. He's smoking a cigarette with the windows rolled up, which grosses me out but also makes me want to smoke. There is no one in the passenger seat, and he isn't holding up a phone. It's a rusty, cream-colored, beat up Crown Victoria, the kind of car my dad used to drive when he still lived in Syracuse. This guy is talking to himself. Debating whether to go inside.

After the funeral, I go out for eight days straight. Emily has a new Adderall prescription, which we crush up and mix with the coke at her boyfriend's penthouse apartment in Armory Square. We barhop, get bored easily, looking for the next best thing. Everyone I run into starts by mentioning Lina, killing my buzz, sending me back to the bathroom with the blend of mostly pure cocaine and bright blue amphetamines, the drip both sweet and bitter.

I keep thinking about the guy in his car at the end of Lina's driveway. Thinking maybe I'll run into him downtown. The latest in a series of toxic relationships that started with Colin, the high school boyfriend who touched her for the first time when she was passed out drunk. This newer guy, though, he knows something none of us know.

It's not like I'm expecting Patrick and Juan to send out a newsletter with the autopsy results. But I do expect there to be new information, something that says this isn't over, a longer epilogue to Lina's story.

———

Lina had a small pool party for her seventeenth birthday, in July, before our senior year. She was always one of the youngest in our class, because she'd skipped a grade in elementary school. I could tell from the decor that Patrick had planned the party: pink and gold balloons tied to the pillars near the entrance, pink streamers over the door, and little gold gift bags in the foyer.

I was the first guest to arrive, and I went to Lina's bedroom to change into my swimsuit. The sun coming through the bay windows filled up the yellow room, making it a golden temple.

"Patrick is doing everything to try to make me not depressed. This party, which no one else is gonna come to. Then they're making me go to Puerto Rico with them."

"Making you?" I asked. I turned away from her to pull my shirt off, hiding my cheap bra, my tiny cone-shaped excuses for breasts. I knocked a hoop off by accident.

"Yeah. I mean PR is cool and all, but I'll miss all the parties right before school starts. And like, I'm already tan."

"Why are you depressed?" I asked, pulling my one piece on before bending over to retrieve the dropped earring.

"I don't know, dude, it's not like, something you can really put a finger on."

"Maybe getting away will make you feel better? I'd love to go to Puerto Rico."

"Come, then."

"Yeah right."

My earring lay between two empty handles of vodka.

Yes, Lina's bedroom was a fun place to hang out, with its 72" huge flat-screen TV and California king bed with the perfect level of firmness, and her two-foot-high stack of DVDs, and the excellent air conditioning. But still. Why was she drinking alone?

"No, seriously, you should come," she said. "Patrick would love it."

Lina took her sundress off. She had a bright orange PacSun bikini on. She had tits and hips filling in, which she said made her look fat. To me, she looked like she stepped off the cover of a surfer magazine. Her skin was glowing, her hair, not gelled or straightened like usual, flowed dark, silky, and wavy around her shoulders. But the skin under her eyes was dark, her eyes crinkled with worry.

I shook my head. "I couldn't afford it."

My eyes found the bright red, wide scars across her thighs. It had been a long time since I noticed any new scars on her arms, and I thought she'd grown out of her cutting phase, like the rest of us had. My scars had already cleared up, the result of dragging sewing needles or safety pins through the shallow of my skin, an experiment in transferring psychic pain to the outside, less extreme than tattoos. Hers were surgical, performed with a knife. Where mine had been scratched skin, barely red, hers had bled, needed bandaging.

"You'll hardly have to pay for anything."

I saw the thread—the red lines, the empty bottles—but I said nothing.

It's a sunny day, but hazy, so the light's more white than golden. The last snow of the year came on Mother's Day, a spring of new lows. Summer's almost official and the trees are still more branch than leaf, hardly any bloom.

They remind me of being fifteen, struggling so hard against those long dark winters to get out of bed for school. I sat alone on the floor by the radiator waiting for the heat to kick in. Lina struggled even more. I remember snuggling under her soft, warm comforter during sleepovers, waiting for her to wake up so we could go downstairs and eat Patrick's beautiful, elaborate breakfast. But she could sleep and sleep, until one or two in the afternoon. And she looked so peaceful, a little smile on her lips, sometimes giggling at dreams.

The house is on the Northside, has dark brown siding, the color of mud. There's a white plastic screen door off to the right, with no steps leading to it, just a stack of cinder blocks serving as a porch. Lina had sent me the address so I could send her a Christmas gift, a little bobblehead Bob Marley I found at an antique shop in Soho. But I never remembered to send it, thinking I'd give it to her the next time I saw her.

There's no driveway, and there's a broken-down old pick-up parked in the yard and that old Crown Victoria in the front.

The blinds on the house are drawn. The snow's melted, but the grass on the yard and along the sidewalk is still patchy and brown. Weeds with yellow flowers struggle to grow in a narrow strip of dry soil lining the front of the house.

A white screen door cracks open, and a pale figure steps out. I put the car in drive, panicked. It's him. I recognize him from the way he smokes his cigarette, sucking the smoke with his lips curled, like he's in a hurry to get to the filter.

I think he hasn't seen me, but then he makes direct eye contact. I wish I was in Lina's car, with its tinted windows. It feels like an insult to be here without her. He waves, smiling. He recognizes me, too—probably knows my face better than I know his. She never posted Facebook photos with him. "Hey," he calls out. I park again, get out of the car.

"Hi."

We don't say our names. Something has already passed between us.

"Come on up," he says, inviting me onto the cinder block steps. Butts smoked down to the filter litter the ground around them.

"This is your house?"

"My mom's," he says.

His smile is a little mocking, his teeth surprisingly white. He finishes his cigarette and lights another with its tip.

"So," I say, not knowing how to raise the topic of the jewelry.

"So, Miss Mari," he says. "Want something to drink?"

I follow him in.

The living room is dark but more or less tidy. A middle-aged white woman and man sit on an old gray corduroy couch, drinking forties of Olde English and watching *The Price is Right* with the volume low.

"This my mom. Her…friend, Greg."

Sean's mother barely looks up, but Greg's eyes linger on me, making me feel the oil coating my skin. It smells fake sweet, like an orange vanilla car freshener.

"Lina's friend."

His mother's eyes float up to meet mine, a shock of blue. "Lina?"

"Lina's *friend*, Ma. Mari."

"Oh…poor Lina," she says, her eyes unfocused on me.

My skin prickles. Sean disappears into the kitchen. It is both dirty and neat in here. Books and papers are organized into stacks on the floor in the corner, and the miscellaneous junk has all been put in a punch bowl on the table. But the light streaming in through the blinds makes visible the thick layer of dust on everything. I think about Lina on that couch, her legs folded up under her, how small she became.

Sean emerges from the kitchen with two Styrofoam cups filled with bloodred liquid.

"Kool-Aid. Sorry, we ran out of beers."

We go back to the cinder block steps.

He looks more well than he should. His hair is dark, with bleached tips, very early 2000s emo band. His eyes are intensely blue-green. He's pale but there's peach under his skin. I smell cigarettes, but no body odor. What is it that's holding him up?

He lights another cigarette, and offers me one. It's a cheap menthol, a Kool, the kind they sell eight dollars for a double pack at the smoke shop.

"Sorry I didn't make it to her funeral," he says.

I find myself sucking down the cigarette the same way he does. "I don't know if her dads would have wanted you there."

He shrugs. "Yeah. I just got out of jail. That day. I was pretty desperate to get high, to be honest."

"How long were you in jail?"

"Three weeks," he said. "Criminal mischief. Got into a little tussle."

I'd been convinced Sean was the one who'd bought the fatal dose for Lina. They'd planned to get high together, but they'd gotten into a fight. Maybe he hurt her. She took what was supposed to be for both of them all to herself.

"I should have been there," he says. "I need a minute," he adds, and retreats into the house.

I am thinking about the jewelry. I think that if I can do this for Patrick and Juan, it will help resolve something, close one scene in this gruesome chapter. I need to find a way to look around the house for the velvet jewelry box, or a pawn shop receipt.

Sean doesn't protest when I follow him inside. He doesn't close the door to the bedroom at the back of the hallway, so I go in too.

He uses a real stone mortar and pestle, the kind Patrick uses to make pesto, to crush up half of one of the small pink pills.

"You sure you want to watch?" he asks.

"I'm curious," I say.

He puts the crushed pill on a metal spoon. My heart races like I'm the one who's about to shoot up. He uses a syringe to extract a vial of water from a bottle on the night stand, and adds the water to the powder in the spoon.

He uses a lighter to heat up the bottom of the spoon.

I remember the summer we started experimenting. We did almost everything we could get our hands on, but Lina avoided uppers. They were too overwhelming for her, her body on overdrive, dopamine and serotonin crashing her system like a hard drive with too many LimeWire downloads. Then she would have these horrible crashes the next day, when she would drink a whole bottle of liquor to quiet her glitching brain.

How long had it taken for Sean to convince her to do this?

He rolls up the sleeve of his hoodie. He tightens a child's belt around his arm, and I wonder whose child it belongs to.

On his forearm, there's a two-inch stretch of dark vein that ends with a mark at the crook of his elbow, a small sore. When he starts to position the needle going directly into the sore, I look away.

"Goddamn it."

"What's wrong?" I try to look at his face, not his arm.

"Can't get it," he says. "Fuck!"

He takes one hand and puts it between his thighs and squeezes his legs together until the veins in his fist swell. I notice little scars dotting his hands.

He finds a good vein. I look at my own hands. I notice the forked road networks of vein, branching off at my wrists and traveling to my knuckles before becoming indiscernible. I think of the time Lina and I took mushrooms and spent hours looking at our hands and each other's. Comparing our shades of brown, how mine was more yellow and hers more red. Noticing the little hairs sprouting up from our fingers. How like paws they were. Marveling at having a body, we promised ourselves and each other we would no longer take them for granted, would never again abuse them.

Sean sighs in relief, then everything goes quiet. I can even hear the game show his mom is watching in the living room. I watch his eyes roll back, then close.

When they open again, his pupils are tiny black pinpricks in his watery blue eyes. He puts the syringe, spoon, lighter, and pills in a Ziploc bag and stuffs it into the top drawer of the dresser. Then he sits back down and nods off.

I take my opportunity, quietly opening the top dresser drawer and starting to rummage, pushing aside old check stubs, junk mail, light bulbs, batteries, cards lost from their decks, and drug paraphernalia. I hold my breath as if this will help block out the disgust. Which of these tubes did he use to tie up her arm?

"You could just say something," Sean says. I try to pull my hands out of the drawer quickly and end up with a splinter lodged deeply in my index finger. Sean smiles with his bright teeth and freakish blue eyes. "If you need to get hooked up."

"No, no, no." I try to resume breathing, sucking on my finger to extract the sliver of wood. I bring up the missing jewelry, expecting to catch him off guard, for him to play dumb.

"Oh, that's long gone," he says. "Someone on Craigslist bought it."

"When did you take it?"

He stares at me with those icy blue eyes. "You got me wrong. I didn't steal it. She took it."

"It was supposed to be for her wedding," I say. My words hang heavy between us.

"Look, I know you don't like me," Sean says. "But I never did her wrong."

"No, no, no." It isn't me who's confused. "You were the one who convinced her to break into the medicine cabinets, to start stealing from her parents. You were the reason she got the DWI. You were the reason Patrick got rid of her car. You know she loved that car. Without it, she was bored to death."

"Listen to you. You really believe that?"

"Believe what?"

"It started with me?"

"You don't know what she was like before you."

"You don't know what she was like before *you*," he says.

"Are you serious?"

"Let's not argue. Seeing you—talking to you—it's the only thing that gives me a little bit of relief. Besides, you know what she told me about you?"

"What?"

"You're the one who gave her her first pill."

I search my blurry memories. Had I?

I dream about Lina. I am trying to convince her that we can find something fun to do sober. Only when I am trying to plan this activity do I realize how hard sobriety must be. Weed and alcohol enhanced everything we did together—rollerblading, movies, the arcade, chilling by her pool.

We've finally decide to go get pizza and wings from Mario and Salvo's when Sean shows up. He ties up her arm with one of those resistance bands they use in group exercise classes. I'm too curious to protest. He strokes the soft skin inside her elbow first, a sad foreplay.

I wake up nauseous but aroused.

I let the missed call notifications and unanswered texts pile up. A few are from my college roommate asking when I'm coming back to the city. A couple are from Lina's high school boyfriend Colin, long rambling messages, full of drunken typos, about how much he loved her. Most are from Aisha, who keeps checking in to ask how I am, and to send me links to poems and articles about friendship and grief.

Sitting in my childhood bed, where I lost my virginity at fourteen, with my T-shirt and leggings, makeup-less, with tangled hair, I scroll through her LiveJournal until my contacts cake over with protein.

How did I miss all the calls for help? Has it been so long since I last logged in? Was I too caught up in college? Had I seen the posts and ignored them, chalking them up to Lina's morbid humor?

I don't blame Heath Ledger for overdosing, Lina wrote in January.

The night before we left for college, Lina and I sat on her plush king-sized bed, listening to Mario's "Let me Love You" on repeat and making lists of everyone we'd ever hooked up with, make outs included. We'd rolled up her Bob Marley posters, untangled and packed the necklaces hanging from the rays of a metal sun mounted against the yellow wall, and sorted her DVDs into three piles: take, leave, and give to Mari. Her room looked even bigger, and brighter yellow, in its bareness.

Lina ran out of names around twenty, I got to thirty-two.

"Now we know who's the bigger slut," I said.

"Don't say that!" She nudged me with her shoulder, shoving me towards the edge of her bed. "One day, these boys will be sending you apology letters. You'll be the one who got away. Meanwhile, I'll just be the depressed loser who's crying when I don't get a text back after the first fuck."

I protested, but she held up her small hand. "Never let a guy mistreat you, OK? I know you won't, but promise. Don't let them hurt you, like I did."

"No, bitch. You didn't let anyone hurt you. They did that. That's not on you. They're afraid that if they don't hurt you, you'll hurt them first. That's fucked up."

"I'm fucked up too." A tear dangled from the cliff of her lower lid. "Don't you get it?" She was looking at me, but past me—into her sadness.

I found my purse, the pill bottle inside. I'd been building up a little stash during my time working as a cashier at the Eckerd's pharmacy, swiping one or two pills per shift. I pulled out two Oxys. One for me, one for her.

I sit in the bedroom at my mom's, which I still don't think of as my bedroom, since she moved me into the smaller room that was once my nursery. My mom keeps telling me to stop calling it her house. That it's my house too. But there are none of my Johnny Depp or Allen Iverson posters. My Model UN gavel awards are all tucked away in the crawl space of an attic.

This time, I want to access her private posts. I run through a series of potential passwords.

LiveJournal is not like the newer sites that make you stop trying after X number of failed attempts. It just lets you keep trying and trying. I find the right password, which means it was buried in my memory all along: jimi315. Jimi her last living Chihuahua, 315 our area code. Too easy. We always shared our passwords, and sometimes pranked our friends by signing into each other's AIM accounts and pretending to be the other.

I'm glad I'm not using drugs and alcohol to cope, she writes. *Before rehab in Arizona, I was smoking every day. To forget. Drinking 'til I passed out.*

Being inside Lina's mind makes me restless. She goes around in circles, from hope to hopelessness, in the space of a sentence, the progression from life to death and back.

I'm still living the consequences of my abusive relationships. I got heavy into drugs and neglected my friends but then again are they really my friends if they couldn't see me through my darkest days? Still I would tell them I'm sorry I fucked up that I bailed or never called back. I was probably somewhere drooling on a couch. But now I'm sober which is good but then all day I think about how hard it is to stay sober. I hope this will be over soon.

When I'm not at my computer going through her entries, I have the feeling a deep conversation has ended abruptly, the cadence of Lina's voice stuck between my ears.

The tiny pills stashed in my jewelry box have been beckoning me for days with their tiny voices. Sometimes I walk into the room and it's like the jewelry box has come alive, it has this pulse of energy around it that makes it glow.

I don't think painkillers is the right word. Opiates don't so much kill the pain as change your relationship to it. You can still tap into the pain, access it, remember it's there. But it sort of blurs, becomes unthreatening. The pain is there, but it doesn't belong to you.

When I close my eyes, I see her slim, arched eyebrows, the mole on her cheek, a tear on her lower eyelid. I hear her chuckle, that laugh so much deeper than her speaking voice.

I wish I could say I flushed the pills down the toilet. That seeing what this drug did to my best friend made me never want to try it myself.

I should take all of it now, and then it will be done, and I won't want it anymore, because it won't be there. This time, it will be different. When I finish these, it's over.

I finally go up to St. Mary's. I bring a spliff with me, mostly tobacco with a little weed sprinkled in, the kind we used to roll when we were on our way to friends' houses and had to interact with parents. I bring two shooters of tequila.

The grass is starting to fill in, but you can still see the rectangle where they lowered her coffin. Now there is a big granite headstone, and colorful tulips grow in dark mulch, yellow and bright pink. There are little clay pots with cacti with orange blossoms, and sugar skulls, and brass angels. It's the most beautiful grave in the whole cemetery.

I tuck the Bob Marley bobblehead I've been holding on to for her behind the headstone. I think she'll find it funny. I pop the top off her shooter and pour out the tequila in the mulch. It can't hurt her now.

I think to say a prayer, but I'm not sure who to direct it to. So I talk to her. I tell her that marriage equality is gaining steam, and soon we'll live in a world where parents like hers can be legal spouses. I mourn, like we used to, for the girlhood of our peers in Iraq and Afghanistan who have come of age during war, and how much easier it has been for us to forget the wars altogether.

"Damn, I miss you. I could use one of our nights right now." Loss is a cruel loop—the one person who can most comfort you, the one person you want to talk to about how much this sucks, is gone.

Patrick greets me at the door, as he always has. His beard is grown out for the first time I remember, and I notice how many grays he has.

The house smells good, like bread baking.

"Where's Juan?" I ask.

"He got his own apartment downtown. We still have dinner together a couple times a week."

I thought about what Lina had said about Juan's other life with a younger man. How she predicted that she was the only thing keeping him and Patrick together. I think she'd be surprised that they still get together. That she's bringing them together, even now.

"Can I have a minute in her room?"

Patrick smiles. "I get it. I go in there when I really want to feel her presence. When I need to ask her a question."

"Yeah. I just want to be with her for a little," I say.

I close the door. I scoot under her bed, find the loose floorboard, pry it up. There's the tin box where she used to keep weed, pipes, lighters. I bust it open.

In it, I find the equipment. A syringe and a spoon. A rubber tourniquet. An empty baggie.

Even though it's what I expected, I can't believe I'm really seeing her kit, putting my hands on her needle. It feels like the ultimate step into her most private, darkest place.

I take the whole box home.

There's no trace of anything on the baggie. I turn it inside out and suck it. No taste. That doesn't mean anything. She could have prepared her shot, flipped the bag inside out, and licked it clean herself. My DNA mingling with hers.

I crush the pill.

I try to remember how Sean did it.

I have more trouble than I could have imagined trying to tie my arm with the tourniquet.

I remember Sean sticking the needle in his hand. I ball up my fist and search for the most prominent vein.

Searching, I suddenly see myself as an animal, I recognize my own paw.

I hear Lina's voice, gravelly from smoking too many Djarum clove cigarettes, our favorite treat while tripping. "After tonight, we're going to realize how precious we are."

Because we looked at each other's hands and saw the beauty there, and the beauty of our own. That intricate network of veins, the tiny geometrics of our skin, those elaborate folds in our knuckles, every ridge of each fingernail.

Because when I go to shoot up, I feel her soft hand covering mine.

Lonely Apocalypse of the Heart

there are gnats in the wine

but we drink it

lipstick smeared

a mess of arms

anywhere you look

there are ancient appetites

which cannot be fed

no food or drink or love

so why not wander into this dark

where the neon beach signs glow

where the drunken silence roars

and make a home of this midnight

this midnight with your eyes closed

where you could be anywhere

but choose to be here

The Fisherman

sailor,

while you were above land,

the ocean was dreaming about your

figure, waiting for you to come into

the dark—then, like a razor blade

buried in your breakfast, it came.

the dark. your mouth. the taste of

blood on a sunday. under

the quiet moon, you pressed

your bare feet into the sand,

stepped into the dark and

the dark stepped into you,

a trembling dog in the night,

never brave enough to be evil,

never strong enough to be good.

Handbook for Demolition Cats

Appendix B: Floor Map of The Demolition Store (E–L)

E.

ESCRITOIRE DESKS . . . . **SECTION(S) 15**

Behind which Mister Vandeleur and Mister Jasper (*see also:* New Owners, or "Parents") sit during store hours. This is when they are not heaving salvaged wares to the freight elevator (26) or walking the floor with customers, discussing the merits of architectural restoration, or debating between them what stands to be gained from whatever this latest old and once-loved estate. Though the computers and printers stationed alongside are warm as body heat, you are not allowed to lie on them.

F.

FOOD BOWLS . . . . **SECTION(S) 1, 2**

Mister Jasper will engrave a dish with whatever your name (*see also:* Naming of New Cats). This may take several days. Perhaps your ragged and red-brick-dusted collar will proclaim you a Peregrine; or your unbrushed coat, the color of rust or peaches, will render you a Garnet, or a Rufus, or Georgia. Or possibly, for a while, you will be Sir Geoffrey, for your dapper tuxedo reflects so nicely in the oversized mirror torn from a (deceased) gentleman's dressing room; until, that is, a customer, a last hold-out on his corner lot, will remember you as Mr. Bopsey, the neighborhood cat. (The toddler who named you has outgrown his stroller, and with his family has moved, months ago, priced well upstate.) Or maybe, somehow, Mister Jasper will know you to be named Muddle, because your First Owner, who proudly served cocktails at Fallston's Smithy, Hadley's most historic bar, came often into The Demolition Store, though always "to look" and never "to buy." Mister Jasper liked her, had thought her a nice girl, and though he learned her cat's name from the photos she showed to him on her phone's spider-cracked screen, he never learned hers, nor her number, nor how to get ahold of her, to tell her he has discovered, wandering in the cold, her darling kitty dear. Now that he thinks of it, he is sure she has not come to browse in something nearing a year.

FREESTANDING DOORS . . . . **SECTION(S) 33, 34, 35, 41, 49, 55, 58**
No matter which you watch or for how long, these doors will not open. Without hinges, leaned against walls, scraped of paint. No one has yet come through any of them, and certainly not for you. Understand early: Your First Owner (*see also*: Family Is Not for Demolition Cats) will never be behind them.

FRONT ENTRANCE . . . . **SECTION(S) 16**
The entrance through which customers arrive, as well as those who look like customers but, in fact, wish for a functional toilet or directions to Montague's Food Event, the public stretch of beach downriver, the Victorian Spa—or else, delivery men who do not yet know to locate the freight entrance (27). Though it may be weeks after your arrival or upward of half a year, this is also the door through which Mister Jasper carries, inside to their beds, and out to various vets, New Demolition Cats (*see also*: Rivals for Affection). Understand that his capacity for love, when it comes to Demolition Cats, can continue to expand ceaselessly. You will not have to learn the limits of *his* love.

G.
GOTHIC WARDROBE. . . . . **SECTION(S) 35**
Young customers without houses wonder about a life in which they possess the means to own something so grand. They envision their routine not just with a vintage wardrobe, but a home. If they remind you of your First Owner enough that you twine against their ankles, they will think a pet is a good first step, but though they contemplate asking at the escritoires if the Demolition Cats are also for sale, they will have signed an anti-pet clause on their lease. Their bravery will fail at the thought of sneaking litter or scratching posts past the vestibule cameras in the early hours of the morning, and after all, they will often be away and still prefer to stay out late, and hardly like to come back to their dark and lonesome little "place," even well past last call.

H.
HALL OF SINKS . . . . **SECTION(S) 50–59**
During your first days at the Demolition Store, you will take turns lying in every basin. If a sink is a housecat's delight, a room full of them must surely be paradise, even though

they are dry as the oxidized fountains languishing in the Statuary Gardens, and there is no one here to make them drip for you.

HEARTHS . . . . **SECTION(S) 38–42**
Home renovators and house flippers will wonder if they have the know-how to situate such heavy carved stone in front of a working fire. These will like you to stand in the frame; it is easy to replace you with an image of their own pets, or their buyers' pets—not Demolition Cats but Salvaged Cats—who they foresee curling comfortably in front of a warm blaze in that same grate. Stay or go; even if their picture becomes a reality, it will never include you.

J.

JESUS ON THE CROSS . . . . **SECTION(S) 23**
Rested on its side on the floor, it shudders under your perched feet like the tires of the car that brought you here along Hadley's cobbled Main Street. When a customer asks to see it upright—taller than Mister Vandeleur as he holds it aloft—it matches the painted crosses that dot the river-rapids' edge, hanging with flowers instead of a doomed man. Like the markers on the rocks, silence eddies with the dust from those anguished boards, and if they do not quickly brush it away while Mister Vandeleur returns the cross to the floor, you might see the water dripping from the customer's downturned gaze.

L.

LANDINGS . . . . **SECTION(S) 19, 31, 43**
You will soon take to sleeping at the tops of stairs. The hard wooden floors, like a hair shirt or cat-o'-nine-tails, will punish you for what you have lost. When you wake, you will discover your sore, matted limbs with a sacrificial pride and each time you slip down the precipitous step, you will know physical pain is easier to endure than a fractured soul. You will prefer this to the bed Mister Jasper will buy specially for you; even though Mister Vandeleur will complain about the wasted expense, the sudden escalation of cats, Mister Jasper will cite concern at your protruding bones and favored limbs, and will suggest a trip to the vet clinic, and to locate the cat carrier, and to hurry.

LEADLIGHTS AND STAINED GLASS CEILINGS . . . . **SECTION(S) 23–27**
Some customers will walk with you down this hall as they would through a museum or cathedral, wondering from which altars the effulgent saints were deposed. What old residence or house of worship now has a gaping hole where its soul had been? Which have already caved upon their foundations? These will begin to see you as some sort of harbinger, they will call you rat catcher of the end of days. And though they will stroke

the colored light spilling across your forehead, whisper, "Here, kitty, kitty," they will do so with fear of the gentle eternity pouring like prayer with your breath.

LIGHTING (EXTERIOR) . . . . **SECTION(S) 60–65**
(*See also:* Outside) To be watched through the screen door. Do not try to run through the customers' legs or manipulate their good intentions so that they hold the way open for you. Do not run for the lanterns razed from oxidized bridges or hide under the cast-iron lampposts, rust flaking down like the rain and snow since your First Owner left you. When Mister Jasper rushes from his escritoire to recover you, you will not smell the cigarette smoke of your First Owner's hair, as she returned home from her alehouse, her long nights out, to hold you in the studio apartment you shared, the streetlamp at the window dimming in the rising light. The salt and spilled cocktail syrup sweet against your tongue as you kissed her welcome hand, you and she were one structure, built into each other's dimensions. You were the core of her, she said; without you, she would crumble. But though you wait, and wait, she will not appear behind *this* door, either.

Happy Birthday

My father shared a birthday with Keith Richards—the same year, the same date—and I thought it would be a good seventy-seventh birthday present if I could convince Keith Richards to dress up as my father: that is, if I could convince Keith Richards to wear pleated khaki pants and boat shoes and a tucked-in striped oxford shirt and, since their birthday was in December and my dad and I lived in a cold part of the world, a fleece pullover, and if Keith really wanted to go for it, a wig, of white hair, combed to the right and a little thinning on top, and then show up at my father's house on December 18 to wish him happy birthday, or if that was too much to ask (and I suspected it was too much to ask), just to send a picture of himself dressed as my father so I could frame it and give it to my father for his birthday. "He's a big fan," I said in the email I wrote Keith. This was not true—I was a much bigger fan than my father was—but I figured Keith didn't need to know this, and besides, even if my father wasn't a big fan, he liked the Rolling Stones' songs just fine, or at least he liked some of the songs, or at least he knew of a few of the songs, a few of the titles, and a few of the choruses, the things pretty much everyone knew. Even so, I knew he'd at least get a kick out of it: my father was well known for getting a kick out of things. He was a happy guy, I told Keith, figuring he'd like to know a little bit about my father, and in fact, I told Keith, in the email, that my father's favorite Rolling Stones song was "Happy," which Keith sang, of course, even though it was not true that it was my father's favorite Rolling Stones song, and in fact it was not even my favorite song, but of course I didn't tell Keith that, either. And I didn't tell Keith that it was probably more accurate to say that my father had been a happy guy, was formerly a happy guy, and that while I could remember very clearly his being a happy guy when I was a child, and his birthdays being very happy occasions, sort of warm-ups or appetizers for the bigger all-over happiness that was Christmas, just a week after his birthday, over the years he'd become a little less happy with every birthday. Not that he was ever unhappy, exactly. It was more that the years seemed to chip away at his happiness, so that with each birthday his happiness became a little, and then a lot, smaller. Earlier, my father's happiness had been something you couldn't miss, it emanated from him, like light, and sound, and was so powerful that it made it you happy, too. But then my mother, his wife, died, and then I moved away, to try to make something of myself, failed, and tried to make something else of myself, failed, trying and failing and trying and failing for years and years until there was nothing I had not tried, nothing I had not failed at, including love. Love was another thing I'd failed at, so said my girlfriend, my last girlfriend, not in so many words, of course, she did not say, "You failed at love, Silas," but she did say, "I don't love you anymore, Silas," which is pretty much the same thing, and which felt like the final failure, the permanent one. And so I moved back home and started bartending at The Renaissance, the bar where I'd worked before I'd tried and failed to make something of myself, the bar where my father had had his retirement party, just six months before his seventy-seventh birthday. Officially, the retirement was voluntary, but everyone knew that as a teacher of Algebra II my dad had slipped some, and that he tended to fall asleep while the kids were taking their tests, and in fact sometimes he gave the kids the same test he'd given them just the week before, and sometimes didn't teach Algebra II at all, but would spend their fifty-five minutes together telling his students about the latest episode of his favorite show, which was *NCIS*, and so while it officially was a voluntary retirement, and at my dad's retirement party all the toasters said how sad it'd be not to have the old guy around, and couldn't they convince him to stay on just a year or two more, everyone knew he was being forced out. My father knew it, too. "I retire a happy man," my father said, but his voice was shaking when he spoke, and he was also sort of bent at the waist, as though he'd just been hit in the stomach. And so with each new blow my father's happiness had gotten smaller, so that by the time his seventy-seventh birthday was on the horizon, you really had to look for my father's happiness, and while you still couldn't say my father was unhappy—in many ways he remained the happiest person I knew—his shrinking happiness made me unhappy. Although I should say that it would be more accurate to say that it made me more unhappy, because by this point in my life I was very unhappy, and one of the things that made me so unhappy was thinking about what my last girlfriend said to me when I asked her why she didn't love me anymore, and she responded, "You don't think about anyone but yourself," and now here I was, scheming to give my father a present that so obviously was much more a present that I would want than my father, a present that I wished someone would give me, and I thought, wow, I am so selfish, and so then, right in the middle of the email I was writing to Keith Richards, I sat there and tried to think of another present for my father, one that he might really want. But I couldn't, the present that I'd already thought of was like a large rock that I couldn't push out of the way to consider all the other possible better presents behind it, and it was then I came to this theory: when we say someone is selfish, we really mean that they've run out of ideas, that they're too tired and defeated and lazy and inward to think of anything other than the first thing they think of, which is themselves, even when it comes to the people they love. Or, in my case, the person they love. And when I realized that, I was even more unhappy, so unhappy that I wished I were dead.

But no, I decided Keith didn't need to know all that.

Instead, I just wrote, *Dear Mr. Richards, my father has the same exact birthday as you. He's a big fan. He's a happy guy, and in fact his favorite song is "Happy." Here's a picture of him. My father and I would love it if you'd dress up as him and then come to his house on your and his birthday, and surprise him, and if that's too much to ask—and I realize it probably is too much to ask—then if you could take a picture of yourself dressed like my father and send it to him, he would love that. Thank you. Silas Barton.*

Then I sent the email. This was in early November. Two days before my father's birthday I knew Keith wasn't going to come through, and so I went out and got my dad another birthday present. I'm not going to tell you what it was. It's the kind of present people give their father when they don't know what to give them. My dad opened it and grinned, like it was just what he wanted, which couldn't have been true. We were both sitting on the couch, but he got to his feet and I got to mine and we hugged each other and he said, "Thank you. I love it." Then my father pulled back, put his hands on my shoulders, and considered me, his eyes tiny and tired-looking and set way back in his wrinkled face. "I know you don't want to be here," my father said, "but I'm glad you are."

Oh, what do you say when your father tells you something like that? "I'm glad, too," probably, or, "Happy, birthday, Dad, I love you." Instead, I said, "I feel like such a failure."

"Get used to it," my father said, his voice suddenly hard. He squeezed my shoulders: the squeeze wasn't meant to be comforting, it was meant to hurt, and it did. Then he let go. "Good night," he said, and then he went off to bed and I did too. When I woke up my father was dead. He'd died in his sleep.

Five days later—after my father had been cremated, after I placed the obituary in the paper, after the memorial service—I heard a knock on my front door. It was three in the morning. I'd just gotten home from a double shift at The Renaissance and was about to go to bed. I peeked out the window. It was snowing, hard, the flakes swirling around the floodlight above the door. There, in the driveway, was a Bentley. There, on the front step, was Keith Richards, dressed as my father—the fleece, the khakis, the boat shoes, he was even wearing the white wig. I should have felt something—happiness, satisfaction, I did it!—but all I could think was, *Where have you been*? Maybe Keith had been busy. Or maybe he'd forgotten when my father's birthday was, even though it was his, Keith's, birthday, too, which actually—forgetting his own birthday—seemed like something Keith would do.

Anyway, Keith was too late, and I wasn't even going to answer the door. I was just going to switch off the floodlight and go to bed. But then I took one last look at him. Keith seemed so forlorn, standing out there in the snow, adjusting his wig and staring at the door like a dog that was just starting to realize he wasn't going to be let in. Or like an old man, five days after yet another birthday and three hundred and fifty-nine days before the next one, if there was going to be a next one, standing on a stranger's doorstep in the snow, and all alone. All alone! And I thought, *What should I do?* And then I thought, *What would my father do?* He would open the door and invite Keith in, that's what he would do; he would tell him to take off his shoes, take off his coat, get dry, get warm, and how about a drink, and how about a snack, and then he would cut up some celery and spread some cream cheese on it, and, since it was an occasion, it was turning into an occasion, he would break out the TV trays, and while they ate their celery and cream cheese they would maybe watch some TV, some *NCIS* if it was on, and if it wasn't on then maybe they would listen to some good music, maybe some of Keith's own good music, my son has all your albums, my father would tell Keith, except that maybe that would make Keith uncomfortable, listening to his music in front of a stranger, not thousands of strangers, which Keith was of course used to, but just one stranger, which was much different, much more intimate, and maybe much too intimate, and so maybe they would listen to someone else's music, or maybe they wouldn't listen to music at all, maybe they would just sit there in silence, happy comfortable silence, and maybe they would even feel a little lucky, to be seventy-seven years old and alive and in the company of someone who knew what that was like, who knew what that took, who had felt the slow steady diminishment of the world, the slow fading away of everything that had ever made you so happy, who knew what kinds of terrors and triumphs and disappointments you had to endure just to get to your seventy-seventh birthday, just to get to five days after your seventy-seventh birthday. "Mr. Richards," my father would say, and Keith would stop him and say, "Mr. Richards is my father, call me Keith," which would sound like "Keef" and so my father would say, "Keef, we're here, we did it, happy birthday!" And then I realized that I would live a long time, or maybe I would live a short time, but in either case, never again would I hear my father say "happy birthday!" to me, and never again would I get to say "happy birthday!" to him. That was a sad thought, that was a terrible thought, and it made me want to die, again, still. But that was my sad thought, it was not my father's sad thought, my father would never have had that thought, and he would have never let Keith Richards stand on the front step in the snow, either. No, he would have opened the door and right away, before inviting him in, he would have said to Keith, "Happy Birthday!" like he meant it, and so that's what I did.

Riptide

The oddly calm pocket between waves
is where a rip current takes shape.

Seduced by the view of open water,
you get trapped in that tricky corridor.

Regret like salt overflows your throat,
when you think how other risks turned out.

Picture a lake and drift with the rip.
Remember you can always float.

Remember you can always float.
Picture a lake and drift with the rip.

When you think how other risks turned out,
regret like salt overflows your throat.

You get trapped in that tricky corridor,
and seduced by the view of open water

where a rip current takes shape:
the oddly calm pocket between waves.

Photo by Ben Katarzynski

postal service

dear lucy did you / fuck the mailman or /
am i making that / up again would you /
forgive if i was / your toothbrush tastes mint /
different lucy who is / that you can tell /

me lucy i won't / lose it like last /
time your face lucy / when you came back /
with the bills and / magazines you were happy /
in a new way / you were bouncing lucy /

i have never seen / that before did he /
lay your hair on / a pile of parcels /
don't be scared lucy / just let me know /
how many stamps did / you slick this time?

Rakes, Kickstands, Freckles

Autumn comes and it feels as though the veins of leaves are speaking to me.
There are jokes between us. We share history.

The old grey wool sweater in my closet becomes a monk to us.
While it hunches up mountains, leaves flicker into my hands and beg me to launch them.

We grow dizzy twisting in low late-day light beams
and lie beside the river tracing one another's lifelines in open palms.

We are timeless together. We could become wild with whiskers any moment,
but instead we bask, rotund and orange. We could even scare death away. If it existed.

New Moon, Halfway to Winter Solstice

Ice is forming on the little swamps on the way to fern hill.

What was a slick clay hillside a week ago,
nearly impassable after so much drizzle,
is now frozen into heaves of helpful crystals.

I walk up the hill, then down it, easily,
as though it were a staircase.

At the base, someone has discarded
a superbly fire-orange pumpkin
upon a heap of garden debris.

The sight of it causes, in my body, a ticking.
(Why can't I always feel like this?)

On my way back to town,
I stop by the graveyard to jot this down,
a raven has just opened its wings,
a luxury of gilded black-blue feathers,
and glided to a stop between two frost-covered headstones.

Must I go, season to season, not writing to you?

What we loved was, and was not, one another.

Oblivion

I was young, ugly, and strange; he was old, ugly, and poor. We met online, in a chat group for a niche sexual fetish.

The reason I visited these chat groups was nonsexual. During the day I bused tables in a high-end restaurant. A manicure was part of my uniform. Most important, I was told, was to present my Best Self at all times. My Best Self wore a small and gently professional smile, which widened inexplicably into a grin when I used my perfect nails to pluck up crusted forks and empty cans and tissues into which guests had deposited their fluids. One day the manager pulled me aside. "Look," he said, "I see that you're enthusiastic, but you've got to stop smiling like that. It's creeping out the guests. OK? All righty then."

Online, there was no need for any illusions.

In the niche sexual fetish chat group, I had started a personal ad. The ad said this:

I would like to experience oblivion, i.e., made to feel as though I no longer exist. If you have a guaranteed method of ensuring this happens, I look forward to hearing from you. No BS please.

Just in case, I attached a picture of my breasts, which are slightly above average size.

I waited three days before checking my in-box. I had gotten twenty-eight replies. I culled out the usual stuff—"looking to fly a young woman 18-29 to my Kenya mansion"—and called the resultant three. The first two didn't pick up. The third rang only once before the receiver clicked, and I heard the slightest inhale before a man's voice said, "George speaking."

We met at a bar. George was diminutive and pale, with the bloated, frightened look that comes over some men as they pass out of their prime. As I approached the table and his eyes locked onto mine, his face visibly fell.

"You must be George," I said as I sat down.

"Yeah. Hey, how old are you, anyway?"

"Twenty," I said.

I heard him inhale a little. "Wow," he said.

"Men enjoy that," I observed.

"Some of us, ha ha," he said. "Others, hey, not so much. Whaddaya know."

I hated small talk. "So how are you going to do it?"

"Listen—hey! Don't talk so loud."

I said, in a slightly quieter voice, "So how are you going to do it?"

"It's—look, have you ever heard of sexual hypnosis?"

"No."

"You don't really have a lot of experience with this kind of thing, do you?"

"Not personally," I said. "Just through browsing."

He snorted. "Browsing!" He took a sip of his beer, one of those dense, lightless stouts that goes straight to the bowel. "You kids—" He stopped himself and cleared his throat. "You—you internet people, I don't understand it."

"You don't have to skirt around the age differential," I said. "It doesn't make me uncomfortable."

That cheered him up greatly. He put a hand on my shoulder and gave it a little awkward, comradely thump before he went on.

"Well, look, I'm an expert hypnotist," he said. "And I can guarantee once I've got you hypnotized you won't even know what planet you're on. Hey, what're you drinking, by the way? Want a drink?"

"No, thank you. Tell me a little more about your experience with hypnotism, please."

"Want to get straight to business, huh?" he said, attempting a leer. The expression had a borrowed, ill-fitting look, like something he was remembering from a movie. Almost before he'd finished saying it, the leer crumbled and he looked terribly anxious, briefly, before his face smoothed out again into roughly the same pleasant-making social face I imagine I was wearing.

"Well—I guess I've been a Dominant for about fifteen years, on account of a natural inclination. I think it's something some guys are just born with and some just—but I won't get into all that—well, so anyway, maybe five years back or so I stumbled onto this hypnosis thing. You're familiar with hypnosis. Well, sexual hypnosis *uses the body to handle the mind.* And vice versa. Basically, using these methods—a mixture of auditory tapes and physical stimulation—I can make you do whatever I want. With your consent," he added hastily.

"I'm not really interested in sex," I said.

He deflated. "Oh."

"I didn't say I was opposed to it," I said. "Necessarily."

He blinked, cleared his throat. "Well, the thing is—it's just sort of a part of the method-ology. We could—I mean, we could start slowly. We'll just see how things progress. And then, I don't know…we could…"

His pulse was fluttering unevenly in his forehead. His cheeks, which had a slack, unfinished look to them, darkened slightly. When he looked at me again, his eyes were transformed, wet and soulful and somehow more open. I had the odd sensation he wasn't looking at me at all, but at some personal and intimate abstraction, an idea that wore my face.

"Maybe I'll just start with the tapes," I said.

"Great," he said. "Great, OK. I'll send you the first recording. Listen to it tonight."

The following night after work I opened the email that contained the first recording. I turned off the light and lay flat on my bed. I lived in a single-room efficiency with a bed, a hot plate, and a bedside table covered in self-help magazines from a long-uncanceled subscrip-tion. Dirty plates and glasses lay stacked just in front of the table to be eventually scraped of leavings and/or washed. As I hit Play, I closed my eyes. George's voice came through a second later—just as I'd remembered it but tinnier, with an echoey, ruminative tone.

"OK, we are beginning your hypnosis treatment…if this goes well, you should be, ah… hypnotized…by the end of this recording. [Cleared throat]. Now let's begin. Are you in a comfortable place? Go on and get yourself comfortable."

George's recorded voice was higher than it had sounded at the bar. Absent his physical presence, I could plainly hear a wavering note that ran through his voice and rendered it somehow essentially unsure. His voice rose and dipped in alternating peaks and valleys of assertion and self-disbelief. As he went on, the tension went out of his voice, and he began to speak more fluidly, increasingly relaxed and self-assured, as though in unconscious sync with the stuff of his monologue:

"I'm going to begin, ah, counting back from ten, and by the time I get to one you will be just…so…comfortable. This will put you in a…a trance state. Now I'm going to…to begin counting. You're going to start by relaxing your toes. Ten…nine…you're getting very comfortable, and now you're relaxing your legs…eight…seven…so comfortable, now moving up through the legs, the hips…six…now through the torso, the waist, the shoulders, just relaxing, relaxing…five…like you're falling into a deep sleep, but you're just…so…four…three…so comfortable, you don't want to move…your entire body is relaxed…two…so comfortable…and one. Now you are in a trance…

You're feeling good, you're feeling so relaxed…just floating under the level of con-sciousness…feeling so good…your whole body feeling very light and pleasant...you're beginning to feel aroused…"

That was enough of that. I shut off the recording and lay there for a moment, only faintly disappointed. Then, after a second, I clicked it back on again and listened through to the end, before rewinding it to listen a second time, and then a third.

George's voice had all the qualities I'd seen in him in person—defensiveness, insecurity, bravado, doubt. But, when disembodied, it seemed like a distilled, truer essence of his char-acter. Not only was George a liar, he was a bad one; it sounded as though the only person he had ever convinced was himself. There was something perversely impressive about this. And so I emailed him back, a curt little message expressing my desire to see him again.

I met up with George the following week to exchange notes.

"Did you listen to the recording?"

"I did."

He leaned towards me. "Did you go into a trance?"

I thought about lying for a second. "No."

He squinted at me. "OK," he said. Then he mumbled something.

"What?"

He spoke a little louder, but not much. "Pineapple," was what he said. Then looked at me quickly, eyes narrowed in assessment.

"I told you it didn't work," I said.

He blew air out of the side of his mouth dejectedly. "There are some minds, I find, that are naturally resistant to hypnotic forces."

"I have a very resistant mind," I offered.

He brightened a little. "Oh yeah?"

"Oh yeah. I'm very contrary."

"That wouldn't help," he said. Already this news was reinvigorating him. The spark was coming back into him; he visibly straightened in his seat. "I mean, I've hypnotized hundreds—maybe even thousands—and there are always a few tough nuts."

"That's me," I said.

"That's not necessarily a bad thing, you know," he said, with a sagacious little frown. If he'd had a mustache, he would have stroked it. He looked at me for a long minute. His face began to soften with curiosity. Before whatever personal question he had could materialize, I intervened.

"So you're a real expert," I said encouragingly.

"Well, I've been in this world for a long time," he said, now sounding world-weary. "Seen a lot, done a lot. I remember, there was this girl—I was about your age, and she must've been around seventeen…"

He went on in this vein for a while. As he spoke about himself, his life, his adventures, his face began to flush, and I saw that I had needled into some pleasurable feeling that subsumed him as he imagined himself to be the man he'd described.

"I've always considered myself to be an adventurer by disposition," he was saying. Four beers in and his voice had deepened to a grave, emotionally resonant baritone. He stifled a burp and excused himself to the bathroom.

While he was gone, I took his wallet from the table and rifled through it. Inside was a driver's license, four different credit cards, a business card for a local money lender, a gift card to Target embossed in a motherly hand, and a punch card from a place called Juice Health Xpress with a single punch in it. By the time he sat down again, and as I got a whiff of his clothes—boiled cabbage, an ineffective deodorant—it was as though I'd seen his whole life. There wasn't anything exceptional about his unhappiness except its difference from my own.

"Listen," I said, "I'd like to try again with those recordings. I think if I really apply myself and buckle down, I can get myself hypnotized."

Things carried on like this for some time. Every week George sent me a recording, which I dutifully listened to and discussed with him the following week. Their ineffectiveness didn't seem to bother him. "You're a tough nut," he kept saying. "A tough nut to crack." The more he said it, the more he seemed to relish this idea, as though increasingly convinced that he was a master hypnotist and I was the sole female immune to his magic.

Questions about my life were easily deflected: George was happiest when talking about the other George, the George-through-a-curtain who had women throwing themselves at his feet at the snap of a finger. It only followed that, next, he began making up ideas about me.

He had this idea I worked as a "waitress" in a "diner," the kind of place in which waitresses were freely groped and ass-slapped, and in which, as in a porno, the work was a thin conceit for all sorts of inappropriate sexual goings-on. And he had another, related idea that I was a "freak," which was not inaccurate, although he had translated it to mean I was a sexual deviant of some kind. He had all these ideas about my sexuality. One day he said it was repressed; the next, he insisted it was "engorged with fear."

Most of all, though, my age fascinated him. "Twenty," he kept saying. "God, when I was twenty—when I was twenty—"

And then he'd stop, cut off by some inexpressible feeling that came over him, a feeling I didn't understand but could feel myself, wet and soft as jellied egg, in his eyes' plea.

———

One night, we had been talking for some time about his "years overseas" when he started getting a crafty look. "If I fucked you," he said, "you'd find out what was going on with your sexuality."

Of everything he had told me, the single-direction current of sexual desire was the only honest thing about George I knew. Sex, therefore, occupied a strange, pure space between us that was somehow central to everything else and gave all the lies a strange, heady earnestness.

"Like if I fucked you in the ass, say," he went on. "And you realized you had a kink. That's what a girl like you needs. You just haven't tried enough yet."

"What does fucking me in the ass have to do with oblivion?"

"And that's another thing. You've got to stop going on about this oblivion stuff, it's just morbid."

"Aren't I allowed to try to get what I want too?"

"You don't really want—you're being morbid. Young women like you, that's perfectly normal. What you need is a good old-fashioned—"

His face had grown red and wet, and he stopped to mop his forehead with his shirt-sleeve.

"Getting late," he noted.

I thought about my apartment, my dishes, my stack of magazines, and dread formed a pit in my stomach.

"Maybe I'll come see your place," I said.

He blinked. "How's that now?"

"Can I come over?"

He looked startled, then, with some effort, gave me one of his signature shakily-deployed leers. "Sounds like a plan," he said.

George lived between an electronics store and a place that sold flawed bottles of perfume at discounted prices. The air inside the walk-up was ripe with dust. He had to shoulder his door open. Inside I could see through to the living room, where a heavy woman in an Orioles jersey sat in front of the TV, eating dry cereal from a mixing bowl with her fingers, flake by flake.

"That's Cousin Magda," said George. "Don't mind her."

"Hey," said Cousin Magda, without looking up from the TV.

George's place was poorly lit and sparsely furnished. The furniture—a couch with a thick-looking floral cover, a coffee table made of a hard-looking, cherry-red plastic, shelves that stood at different heights against the walls—had the faded, mismatched look of thrift store finds. There was a smell of creosote and something heavier—the complexly pungent, unmistakable smell of neglect.

At the end of the cramped hallway George shouldered his door open.

"This is my pad," he said. "Ha."

His bed sat in the back right-hand corner. Next to the bed was a small bedside table. On the table was a stack of magazines—the one on top was covered in weight loss advertisements—and a cheap-looking lamp. There was a rack of clothes and a stack of boxes—and that was all.

Next to his bed was a pile of dirty plates and a glass clouded with fingerprints.

"Sorry," he said, following my stare to the plates. "I eat in my room."

"Me too," I said.

"You can sit on the bed," he said. "Sorry there aren't more chairs in here."

"That's OK," I said. I sat gingerly on the bed's corner. George had gotten very quiet and subdued. He stood there for a second, hands playing nervously around his waistline, and then left the room. He came back moments later carrying a bottle.

"I'm going to have some of this," he said to me. "You can have some if you want, too. Or don't, I don't care."

"I'll have some," I said. I could not shake the feeling that I had re-entered my own life, twenty years later, and found it unchanged.

It was some kind of dark liquor that settled jaggedly in the throat. After fifteen minutes or so, George's anxiousness seemed to be fading. A flush came into his face, and whenever he glanced at me his expression was alternately bullying and preoccupied.

"I don't understand it," he said at last.

"Understand what?"

"You know, you're really not so bad-looking," he said. "If you'd only have a little respect for yourself, you might go far."

He looked puzzled when I started laughing, then angry, in that flushed drunk way. "What? What did I say?"

"Nothing," I said. "Never mind."

He didn't seem to hear me. He was shaking his head. "I mean, Jesus," he said. He sighed and let his head drop and hang there. I studied the back of George's neck—marked with soft parallel wrinkles, fuzzed with hairs. At his neck's base, by his collar, I spotted a vulnerable-looking mole.

"I just want to know how a girl like you got to be so—so hopeless," he said.

"Hopeless?"

He shrugged. Then, looking resigned, he reached over and put his hand on my right breast and squeezed, the way old women squeeze fruits in grocery stores to see if they're any good.

———

Afterwards he fell asleep. I slid over his pale flank, dressed quietly, and went outside.

After the claustrophobia of George's apartment, I was stunned with brightness. I stood there, blinking furiously, as I waited for my eyes to adjust. Involuntary tears rolled freely down my face, into my collar.

I walked across the street to the little park on the corner, where two kids, maybe eight or nine years old, were pushing themselves back and forth on the swings. As I watched, one of them leapt off the swing at the height of its arc and fell to the ground like a sack of cement. The child looked up and around, briefly shell-shocked, and then burst into tears.

The other kid dragged his feet in the mulch to stop his swing and ran over.

"Why'd you do that?" I heard him ask.

"Dunno," said the other kid, sniffling.

"Are you OK?"

The kid wiped his nose and nodded. In a minute they were up again, chasing each other around the swings.

I thought then that maybe I'd go back to George's apartment after all. First I would hurt myself somehow. The worse, the better. If a car came at the right moment—I had a fantasy of dragging myself back into his dark little room, bloodied and filthy beyond recognition. Both of my eyes would be blackened, my lips swollen into near-deformity, any remaining hair burnt off or frayed. I would be in such a shape one could not help but help. I would draw his own redemption out of him, unbraiding his conscience from everything that obscured it.

I turned and began to walk slowly, considering. Maybe it was not too late to save each other. Thinking this, I was possessed suddenly by a wild buoyancy. A wind came down the street and sent everything rippling into motion. The trees quivered and shook and threw coins of light. Littered trash—crushed soda cans, greasy fast-food wrappers, empty cigarette packs—whipped into tall columns before skittering back to the pavement. Everything seemed heightened, porous, malleable. Then it hit me: I was in love.

The Fern Cliff (II) (Monazite)

The demotic, "slept better" we say: muffled exhalation of chloroplasts: you & your ideas of altitude & acceptance, *point of view* indeed: the sharp part with its traces of pigment: let's try the balm of amplitude: desire for a debtless voice: privet, wisteria, Russian olive quickening now, the trillium still dreamlike hospitals: bandage me, for I have carved my name & my desire in the maple's haunch: when the professor of Renaissance literature asked me—demanded—is it about *sex,* or is it about *God,* & I answered "Yes": & more besides, but that will do nicely, for getting on: as the English say: the *about:* always twittering from the veiled sthenosphere: & these delicate instruments! our bodies! intercepting the transmissions: we are such gossips: tests of the sedimentary layers agree, the bleach, the dyes, more complex aedicules in silt built up against the bank: what we call the bank: but which we might as well refer to as shoulder, or limit: all the little hospitals where acceptance tarries: have you read its brutal edicts, 2,000 auditors beneath the pavilion of inverted enterprise: sublime economy: my great-great-grandfather gathered heavy crystals from just such a stream, rare mineral he thought would buy his family: out of poverty: that fired industrial lamps in distant factories: boom & bust, his sluices brittle against the compound narrative: & the little fires, set on the brink of unity, the commons: I scavenge nothing from the path: where, in less than one month's time, galax will appear: & flower: this is the part of the song my soul knows best, & trusts least: what does *public* mean: misapprehension of some key verses from, say, the Psalms: we were told not to build a temple here, & yet we tarried: "a nice place" we say: set off, set aside from fleshly burdens: shot through now with plastic residue:

The Fern Cliff (III)

withdrawing into the flash of the transient:
what is *allowed,* vs. what is *ruin:*
are both a function
of slowness, that is, of the dilation of time:
rather than, say, the scaffold
of the river, & its black cache of used tires:

but you don't *look*
like a redneck, the waitress told me:

shaft of embodiment
the breath leans towards: & away from:

Mama the Witch Doctor

I sit at the kitchen table pricking at the legs of my sister's
Barbie doll with a pin, hoping to hear a loud "Owww!"

come from upstairs. I ask my mama what she knows about voodoo
as she throws a chicken foot into my daddy's morning coffee.

I tell her that I wanna learn about black magic, about a history
rooted in something other than a White Jesus and Negro

spirituals. She giggles at me and asks why I think voodoo
isn't rooted in Negro spirituals as she begins humming to the tune

of "I Put a Spell on You." Now of course my daddy steps in
asking why in the Hell I'd want to be rooted in anything

other than Jesus anyway, so I ask him why in the Hell
the blackbird wanted to fly. Mama stirs some cream

and sugar into his coffee, a little bit of salt, and neither of us answer
each other's questions because, if there's one thing you should

know about me and my daddy, it's that neither of us ever wins.
Mama looks at me and says she doesn't believe in "voodoo."

She takes the Barbie doll, throws it in the trash, and tells me
that just 'cause something is misunderstood don't make it evil,

that's White Jesus nonsense. My daddy sits in his chair
stirring his coffee with the chicken foot, chuckling.

Kintsugi

SCR *Series in Latin American Translations*

Kintsugi *is the Japanese tradition of repairing broken pottery with gold, so the gold shows through the cracks.*

The beast, my mother, my love.
MARGUERITE DURAS

Ever since I was a young girl, I suffered from insomnia, and sometimes I think it was on purpose. I knew that if I asked, my grandmother would tell me her stories while she caressed my long, soft hands. "They are dolphin fins," she told me, so different from her thick and cracked hands. Those caresses prepared me for this moment, when I write her story. Our story. My story.

My grandmother, my mother, and my brother go by the same first name. Only I have a different one. My grandmother was first recorded as Yesabhel, but the woman who brought her to Lima was ashamed of that name, misspelled as it was and that of a biblical prostitute, so she recorded her in the national registry as María López Quesquén. Her paternal surname and birthday were dreamed up because no one knew who her father was or when she came into the world. Her own mother had tried to survive, back in the '40s, by looking for a man who would take care of her children and stay by her. They all left her. She and her five children of different fathers lived in a cane shack in the middle of a war zone and black market for petroleum.

My grandmother, who was the oldest daughter, was lucky compared to her siblings. That was what the woman, her "godmother," said when she brought her to the capital and one of its most exclusive districts. She had a three-story house, with a large garden and swimming pool. Since my grandmother was considered family, she never received a salary for cleaning, washing and ironing clothes, cooking. Or for watching the children. Her godmother merely gave her change to donate for Sunday mass.

My grandmother made a huge effort to recall her childhood. Some days she would suc-
cumb to amnesia. Others, when her gaze was lost in the gray Lima dawn, she would tell
me about her childhood. About seeing her neighbor, a boy, lose his arms in an explosion
when he was playing with a grenade he found outside his house. About hunger so intense
that she satisfied it with the smells from other people's kitchens. About her mother, who
tied her to a chair when she went to work and returned to find her passed out, smeared
with feces and urine.

Sometimes panic silenced her voice as she relived those stories. She took years to answer
whether she hated her mother. She said no. "Thanks to her I knew that I would always
take care of myself by myself and would never abandon my daughter."

My grandmother had to finish her housework quickly so that she could take the afternoon off and go to public school, which she attended until third grade. From then on,
her life would be tied to the kitchen, where everything she knew was learned on the fly,
with the energy and curiosity of a girl who survives. "Cooking is pure invention," she
asserted with conviction uncommon for her. The kitchen was her prison, but also her
escape, her art.

At the age of eleven, she met the love of her life in the same house where she worked.
They had brought him from Celendin to work as a mechanic. The godmother had a repu-
tation for collecting only blue-eyed, white children. Since the time they were young, the
two loved each other although everyone had been opposed. The godmother said he could
do better: "How can you settle for a servant?" She paid for private school and English
academy. She found him a job at the yacht club. That is how he saved up to travel by ship
from Callao to Southampton, England. He never returned. My mother was one year old.

To curb Mom's persistence, my grandmother assured her that her father was the man
in the photo pasted on the wall of their twelve-square-foot room. Later, in school, Mom
would recognize the face of singer José Luis Rodríguez and, very thrilled, assure others that he was her father. She got into a fight with those who made fun of her and was
suspended from school. The godmother apologized—"Her mother is an ignoramus," she
claimed as she set things right.

Not only did she allow Mom to stay in her house, she grew very fond of her. She
took her to events at the country club, the social center of the Lima aristocracy that
hosted politicians and international artists. "She looks just like Shirley Temple," they
said, and the godmother swelled with pride as if it were her own child. Her friends
adored Mom's whiteness and green eyes. Surrounded by wealthy people, she became
mesmerized by their elegant clothes, so different from her own mother's. That story
made me think of *Child Star*, an actress's autobiography, that told how when she was

twelve, a film producer promised to make her the biggest star in the world…while showing her his penis.

Not long ago, my grandmother gave me the only photo she had of my grandfather. She asked me to keep it because Mom would throw it away if she found it. "When I come to visit, show it to me. Sometimes I forget his face." She told me, somewhat embarrassed, that he read in English and she burned with envy, because she was not given the same opportunities. More than once she tore apart his books in a sudden fit of frustration.

She never married or had another partner. When I asked her how many men she had been with, she replied curtly, "Just one, because I didn't want to be like my mother."

Mom hit me. If I didn't do homework, *smack*. If I did, and made a mistake, *smack*. If I talked back when she yelled at me, *smack*. If I didn't answer, *smack*.

I always sought comfort in my grandmother. She gave me a spritz of orange blossom water while she caressed my hands and treated me to a story. Like the one about her worst beating. She kept her allowance under her mattress, dreaming of saving enough to buy a ticket for the amusement park rides. One Sunday in summer, after receiving communion, she ran nonstop to the flying chairs. The carousel started to move and the screaming began. All were clinging to the bars. She closed her eyes. She still tasted the host on her palate. She took a deep breath and thought, *Sweet Lord, give me the power to fly*. The chairs revolved at a higher speed. She smiled and moved her arms, imitating the flapping of a bird.

The godmother waited for her at the carousel's exit, squeezing a leather strap in one hand and Mom in the other, wailing in the way of terrible twos. "You are first in line to open your legs, but last to take care of your daughter!" She struck her on the head and back. "So that you learn not to abandon your daughter! And not be like that whore your mother!"

When Mom turned six years old, the godmother decided not to send her to public school. She was afraid some envious child would scratch her little face. She enrolled Mom in the nearest private school run by nuns and paid all the expenses for her education. At school, Mom bragged about her house with a pool. On one birthday she invited play-mates to her house and her godmother received them and gave them sweets for coming to the party. "Is she your mommy?" they asked, and she nodded. "And this is my house." My grandmother, holding a tray of snacks, watched the scene without contradicting her daughter. She spent the rest of the afternoon in the kitchen, staring at her rubber sandals. She confessed to me that that was the hardest blow Mom ever delivered.

Despite what I would have expected, my mother got along well with the godmother's children. Living in a house where her mother was a maid didn't bother her. She invented the game *Who Sleeps More* to quietly slip into the godmother's room while everyone was asleep and try on her jewelry and heels, posing in front of the mirror. My grandmother kept watch so her daughter wouldn't be discovered.

My insomnia is also hereditary.

Every night, my grandmother gave Mom a glass of warm milk with Valerian to make sure she would sleep soundly and not hear the godmother's husband knocking on the door. Just as in colonial Lima, the master did not distinguish domestic from sexual service. One night she waited for him in the laundry room with a pointed knife. He backed away, amazed at her boldness. They wrestled, and my grandmother sliced his forearm. The master told her to go away, that she was an ungrateful piece of shit. My grandmother threatened to reveal the family's secrets: the shirts stained with lipstick, the bank deposits to the woman from the jungle who worked in the bar he frequented in downtown Lima, the envelopes with money for the police and his political party. That was the last nocturnal visit of the master. Every night, my grandmother watched over her daughter's sleep and prayed to her statue of the Virgin Mary. "Beautiful Virgin, watch over her. She is already budding. Let nothing happen to her."

All conversations with my grandmother ended with the same refrain: that I study hard so as not to be a dumbass like her. Her dream had been to study nursing. When the godmother was diagnosed with diabetes, my grandmother suggested taking a Red Cross injection training workshop in order to take care of her. The godmother agreed on the condition that she neglect neither the house nor childrearing.

Soon after, she began to administer injections at home. She was thrilled to finally have a paying job. She spent her money on Scott's Emulsion and vitamins for Mom. But leaving the house made her increasingly nervous. She was afraid of blackouts and car bombs, curfew, and the possibility of another earthquake. Something or everything on the street seemed to remind her of childhood in a war zone. It was the '80s, and the terrorist attacks ended up shattering her nerves. Mom said that she had always been a scaredy-cat and drama queen. "She enjoys suffering."

Many nights, my grandmother woke everyone up insisting that somebody was trying to enter through the terrace roof. They searched, found nothing, and went back to sleep. They would say anything to calm her, and didn't mention the incident. A few days later, the same thing. One morning she called the police at dawn and woke the whole block with the same story: a man had crawled in through the roof. Scandal and shame—there had been no one. She never left the house again.

———

Mom had no shortage of suitors. The godmother launched a screening process as if it were the eighteenth century, which was thwarted when Mom went on vacation to Cajamarca. At the time, five thousand had disappeared, victims of terrorism, in Ayacucho. My grandmother tried everything to prevent her from traveling. She shrieked, sobbed, bleached Mom's favorite clothes. "It was the first time we had been separated," she told me.

My mother traveled. And she came back pregnant.

The godmother was disappointed that she came out with her Sunday Seven and with the only brown-skinned man in Cajamarca, but consoled herself that at least he had money.

Dad already had a daughter and, with my brother, he had completed "the pair." When Mom was pregnant with me, he rejected me and abandoned us. It was not in his plans to have two children with her, especially if one was female. He returned after a few years to avoid legal trouble. One afternoon I overheard a conversation with his friends:

"Married...and with two children. *In the blink of an eye.* How does it feel, friend?" asked one, patting him on the back.

"How can...as if they shot a bullet in your leg. It doesn't kill you, but you're lame your whole life."

Mom worked in the most important bank in Lima. She started out as a clerk and rose to head of the treasury, until the institution went bankrupt due to high inflation in the final year of Alan García's government. Dad was happy with the news because she could finally devote herself to his children full time. He bought her a sewing machine and enrolled her in a tailoring course that she never attended. We used the sewing machine as a table to do homework while she napped every day from two to five in the afternoon.

With her severance pay from the bank, Mama thought about buying a van. She deposited a thousand dollars in a very popular financial advising firm that promised to double your investment in a year. She deposited every bit of her earnings and her savings. Initially, she received fifty percent interest for referring several acquaintances. But after two years, the government had to intervene and dissolve the company. I distinctly remember when she found out she had lost all of her money in that Ponzi scheme, the largest in the history of Peru. It was hard to tell if she was upset or sad—her face was rigid, her tears ran silently down her cheeks.

Without money or work, Mom signed up with various employment agencies. Dad was the sole provider in the family, and he often threw that in her face. Hers and ours. Recently, in the year 2000, she found work as a makeup consultant for a catalog company.

On the weekends, Mom would go out with her friends, my brother would sleep at some friend's house, and Dad would get drunk. My grandmother and I watched movies from the Golden Age of Mexican cinema. One Saturday she took me to the video rental store and let me choose the film. I was very moved by a sleeve of two beautiful women smiling in front of a road that disappeared into the horizon. I desired, with all the power a seven-year-old girl can have, to travel that infinite road and never return.

Let's keep going, Thelma told Louise. *You sure?* asked Louise. The bedroom door opened, but neither of us turned. He smelled of whiskey. Thelma and Louise kissed.

"Gross! What are you doing watching those whores? Do you want to turn my daughter into a whore?" Dad staggered and turned off the television. My grandmother helped him sit down, and he fell asleep instantly.

"Grandma, what is a whore?"

"Whore? A word invented by men."

My most important memories are of liquids. The mesmerizing ripples of the water in the pool, the scent of chlorine drying on my skin, the muffled sound of my heartbeat underwater, the tears that choked me while I swam. You have to swim a lot before you are able to write.

The day the teacher lined up the children going from the baby pool to the twenty-five-meter pool, many ran to hug their mothers on the deck. I broke out of line, grabbed a kickboard and jumped into the pool. I kicked hard to stay afloat and didn't emerge for fifteen years. I wanted to quit swimming many times and have a normal adolescence, but Mom forbade me. "Do you want to be mediocre?" Her pressure was such that it was impossible for me to discover who I was outside of a pool. Even today I feel like a fish out of water.

My grandmother soothed my desolation with seven-seed-grain cookies that she packed for my five a.m. practices. One day she told me, "Be patient with your mommy. You have everything she wanted." She told me that my mother had been a very agile girl who excelled in athletics and once won the gold medal in a national competition, that she was even offered a scholarship. But she had forbidden Mom from accepting it: "Find your own opportunities. Don't accept favors from anyone," she had told her.

I have always felt my mother's rejection in my navel. If I came home drunk one weekend, I was an alcoholic and a whore "because my brother, being a man, didn't go out as much as I did." When, at eighteen, my brother wrecked the car for drunk driving, Mom blamed his friends for being bad influences and, as it was taking too long to repair, she bought him a car of his own so that he could go to college, where he was expelled for repeating the same course three times.

I was the first in the family to complete a professional degree. When I asked Mom to help me with the requirements for the degree, she yelled at me that I had everything easy, that if I wanted a favor, I had to pay her. My grandmother confessed that she did not react well when Mom graduated from the Banking Institute. When Mom eagerly handed her the diploma, she said, "So? What do you want me to do? Throw a party?"

Mom was outraged: "Yes, it would be good, because I'll get a job at a bank and I'll never be a servant like you!"

When I asked why she didn't congratulate Mom, she replied, "I felt like she was moving away from me…that a degree would take her away."

Mom ignored me every time I asked about her life. As if by not naming it, reality ceased to exist. I only know what she has tried to believe happened. Events as historical incidents, with no emotions to explain them. For her, feelings are garbage. A waste of time.

When she taught me how to drive her Toyota Starlet automatic, she repeated with absolute conviction that it was only necessary to shift to D for Drive to accelerate and to brake when I wanted to stop. When I asked her about Neutral and the other gears, she claimed: "They don't work. Do everything in Drive." That was my mother. On autopilot through life.

During summer break after my freshman year of college, I enrolled in a photography class. Mom lent me her Canon EOS-3 camera. She explained that taking a photo was like hunting an animal. "Your weapon is your camera. You have to spot the animal in its environment. You look for an unfamiliar image that speaks to those who see it." Mom smiled as she spoke. She looked beautiful. I didn't recognize her for a moment, spellbound by a passion she never revealed. The photographs she took in her youth slept in a box in her closet, like a clandestine lover. When I asked her why she hadn't exhibited her photos, she said it wasn't that easy. "You have to have important connections or a street named after you."

In class I couldn't keep my hands steady when I held the camera. I was afraid I would drop it or break a button, and Mom would get mad. I stopped attending classes and started visiting exhibits, imagining the stories behind each photograph. There were plain portraits of men and beautiful women. I didn't like their expressions, I don't know why. The photo that I liked most was a rural landscape. The green hills and fields, the turquoise sky. An adobe house in the background. A girl with cracked skin, crusty nostrils, straight hair blowing in the wind. She was not smiling, not posing. She gazed straight at the camera. For some reason the girl reminded me of my grandmother. To see her there, back then, and me here, like this…I don't know. Something shot through me, something forced me to write.

———

Virginia Woolf said that she needed to write down her moments of being, those events that marked her life through the shock, violence, and horror they produced. She said that explaining them on paper blunted the force of the blows, and the ability to survive those impacts made her, in turn, a writer.

Shocks, impacts, moments of being. Where to begin? With the first one, Samael, the son of Dad's best friend. It had been in his head since he was young that I would be his girlfriend. Dead set on fulfilling his intention, whether it was conscious or not, he chased me around the house at family gatherings, forcibly kissed me on the mouth, and when I managed to escape, he would yell at me to come back, that I was his. The adults laughed, moved by our antics. They commented, "But how adorable, these kids!"

He was thirteen and I was five. At a family lunch, he locked me in the bathroom. He covered my mouth and stood behind me. A bulge forcefully rubbed against my back. I was repulsed by the smell of epazote and his moans, the saliva from forced kisses on my neck and face. I felt the pressure of him like a knife and it left an invisible wound that did not heal over time.

I told Mom about it twice. First, at eighteen, when she wanted to host Samael at home. "Don't be a drama queen, those things happen, they are child's play." Then, at thirty, when my grandmother confessed that her godmother's husband had abused her. That time I confronted Mom. "Don't mix things up with Samael," she interrupted me, and her denial was fierce. "In my godmother's house, such a thing would never happen."

My grandmother's erratic behavior deteriorated just around the turn of the millennium, when the internal conflict ended. By then, she was used to wedging a chair against her bedroom door and sleeping with a knife under her pillow. She was sure a man was stalking her. At first, I believed her. I asked her what was he like, when did he stalk her, what his intentions might be. One weekend I spent the night with her. At midnight she woke me up to show me her stalker. "Don't you see him? He is standing there, by the window." She pointed to the building across the street. She was looking at me impatiently, like a child begging to be believed. I blinked several times. I swallowed to stop from crying.

I explained the situation to Mom, but she assumed it was progressive blindness. "She has always been a hypochondriac, I'm sure it's glaucoma." Mom only took her to the psychiatrist after an indisputable psychotic break. One dawn, my grandmother ran out naked and screaming that she'd been raped by a man with the head of a pig. Her private insurance did not cover any antipsychotics or antidepressants, so they only prescribed sedatives. When I called the state mental hospital, they gave me an appointment for five months later. How many more psychotic breaks could she have in that time?

She was diagnosed with incipient schizophrenia. Her lack of sleep depleted her. Her cheeks were sunken, and her false teeth became more prominent. Glaucoma turned her corneas white. She waited for my visits, sitting by the window, smiling, her face lit up by the television's reflection. The sweetest face I ever saw in my life now scared me. She told her visions only to me. Mom forbade her from telling, and no one else visited her, so every day she phoned to tell me about her rapist, the pig-headed man, how he appeared in the bathroom skylight to watch her bathe, how he haunted her bed at night, waiting for the moment she fell asleep to rape her. I listened to her attentively, with the same wonder as when she curled up with me in her bed during my nights of childhood insomnia. Sometimes I held my breath and covered my mouth so she wouldn't hear me drown in sobs.

When I can't sleep, I also imagine the pig-headed man.

I detach myself in unlikely situations. I learned to dissociate from reality to not see the blows between my parents, to forget the slamming doors and the words thrown like knives. Only in that way did I manage to understand that we would later attend mass together, like a normal family.

Rarely did I get a full night's sleep when I lived with my parents. One night, Mom's screams woke me up. I got up and saw her crouching, protecting her head from Dad's blows. My brother stepped in, covered her, and ended up on the floor, trading kicks and punches with Dad. In shock, I grabbed the first thing I saw, a vase, and smashed it against the wall.

Days later, my grandmother pieced it back together. "I fixed it. And now I like it better. I mean…I understand it better. When I touch it, I know exactly what it is." She took my hands and my mother's hands and placed them on the vase.

The three of us caressed the cracks, following the lines to the same beginning.

Translated by Susan Ayres

Amanuensis: Notes on Mann's *Doctor Faustus*

Contrapuntally, you enter a few steps behind, expositing
on your favorite theme, that of your friend's genius.

Call me a child of my age, but though you try
to baffle us with a youthful assignation

or by mentioning your "dear wife," we're drenched
in the homoerotic. The chasm between your passion

for your beloved composer
and the mother of your children gapes vaster

than that between Chopin's nocturnes
and Beethoven's most clamoring dissonance.

Look, man, you follow him town to town,
attend classes that don't interest you, crisscrossing

entire cities just to stay shoulder to shoulder.
No matter how many voices color

your orchestration, *his* sounds loudest,
and in the rests, your pulse, *allegro vivace*.

Donation

Goodbye to how you clung to my neck and spine
after a shower, dark and slick as oil,
glazed with steam; after I washed you
and wrung you as a well that held the rain
of twelve months and a few more. Goodbye
to how you only tangled in the bitter wind
by the sea and nowhere else, but really
how you grew long and fell still as a curtain,
combed with sunlight for good measure,
and undersides that gleamed copper and bronze, even
the occasional thief of white I never caught.
Some mornings I curled you or straightened you
or one after the other because I am just like that,
I loosened you from your ache and sleep, I
tamed you, but you let me, nuzzling the ribbon of skin
behind my ears. Now, parted and cut,
my head already lighter, you will belong
to a little girl who does not look like me.
Goodbye then; I drew you like water into my hands,
I always, like a child, released you.

The Dead Goldfish: A Russian Love Story

for Alexander Vasilyevich

Dear Swedish Migration Board!

The name in my passport reads Lubov Mikhailovna Sverdlova, but you can keep it and the red book that holds it. I stopped considering myself a Russian thirteen weeks ago, when a missile struck the central market in Grozny while I was shopping there with my good friend Makka.

I can't say with any certainty where the missile landed. I didn't return the next day and join the women praying over the scorched crater. But I'm told it was in the area of the open market where you could buy wrenches and hammers and reach into open buckets of nails, and this I have no reason to doubt.

When I pushed myself up from where I'd been thrown by the blast, I saw my friend sitting against the side of the shop's stall, a wall of colorful *khalats* hanging above her. A nail had pierced Makka's cheek, directly beneath the right eye. Her whole face fell away from it, like a crooked painting hanging on the wall.

I said her name two or three times, but still she stared at me with that same fixed expression. Then, praise be to Allah, she blinked.

"This is ridiculous," said my wife Dasha, lowering the letter she was reading from and looking across the table to her father. "*Praise be to Allah?*"

We were sitting in the kitchen of the same St. Petersburg apartment that she'd called home before I'd come here on a Fulbright and married her one drizzly summer afternoon almost eight years ago. Her father sat beside me at the small table pushed up against the wall, a large rocks glass set out in front of him. He reached for a bottle of *samogon* (what my relatives in Texas would've called moonshine) and poured a shot for me and a double for him. Luba's boyfriend stood at the door to the balcony smoking. With his shaved head

53

and sleeveless shirt and black Adidas sweatpants, he was the exact type of Russian that I had always been sure to avoid on the street.

"Keep going," he said. "It gets better." He had come here hoping to find Luba. They had fought a few nights ago, but he hadn't thought anything of it or her absence until he'd found this letter in the tray of their printer this morning. He had come here hoping to confront her with it, but instead he'd discovered only us. Now he stood by the door to the balcony, blowing smoke into the room.

Dasha looked again to her father, a massive man whose weight was somehow supported by the table's tiny chair. "More?" she said. He closed his eyes and frowned, giving his oldest daughter the slightest nod of his head. *Continue.* And so she read:

> I found a bearded man in a camouflage jacket who agreed to drive Makka to the hospital. But as soon as we got there, we found it filled beyond capacity with the dead and the dying and without any electricity besides. Believing we'd have better luck in the country, he drove us next to Achkoy-Martan, but before we could get there I realized it was too late. Makka sat in the back of his small car, wide-eyed and staring, her last breath expelled I don't know how many kilometers ago.
>
> The bearded man parked on the side of the road and reached for my hand and squeezed it. "Look at her," he said, "and tell me what you will do because of it."
>
> I had come to Grozny from my father's native land to grow stronger in my Muslim faith. But it seemed I could not concentrate on the religion that had been given to me by my mother. I had no choice. That night, after a tearful parting from my cousins, I left with the bearded man for a cabin high above the Sunzha River, where for the next several weeks we ate only tins of carp and cans of stewed beef while I learned how to shoot and clean an M82 rifle.
>
> It was this rifle I was holding when I killed my first Russian soldier and claimed allegiance to Shamil Basayev. It was this rifle I was holding when I earned the nickname of "The White Stocking Sniper" and was later captured and raped by an outfit of Russian devils high in the hills above the Grozny suburbs. Let me tell you of the many horrors I suffered, for it is because of this that I will never be safe in Russia again.

"Enough." My father-in-law said this slowly, then drew in a long breath through his nose. "Enough," he repeated, and now he reached for the bottle of *samogon* and poured another for him that was twice as tall as the one for me.

"So none of this is true?" asked Luba's boyfriend.

My father-in-law merely blinked at him. This is how he treated all idiots.

"Is my sister a Chechen terrorist?" said Dasha. "Your girlfriend of six months? Of course not. She is a fabulist, like Gogol. She only wants a better life in Sweden." She asked the boyfriend if he had found the envelope as well, perhaps one already addressed to the Swedish Migration Bureau. "Who knows where she is. But if she hasn't sent it—"

My father-in-law was shaking his head. "This is not the sort of thing one delivers through the mail. This"—he pointed at the letter she was still holding—"this is just a copy she left behind. For us." He looked again to the boyfriend, telling him she'd wanted him to find it and bring it here. "She wanted me to know."

My wife reached for her phone, a primitive Nokia she kept in Russia for those times we came to visit, and dialed her sister's number. The boyfriend had tried her repeatedly this morning, but she hadn't ever answered. It was different for her sister, though. She picked up on the first ring.

"Lube," Dasha said. "Misha just came over with your letter. What's going on? Where are you?" My wife cocked her head to one side, listening. "But why?" More silence, then: "Da." Then: "Da-da-da." Then: "But Lube!"—and now she pulled the phone away from her ear, flinching as she would whenever someone slams a door.

"She hung up?" I asked.

Dasha nodded.

"And?" This came from her father.

"She's in Sweden," Dasha told us, shrugging as if we should've known.

Lubov Mikhailovna Sverdlova had been born in the winter of 1991, just days after Gorbachev had balled up the Soviet Union and thrown it away. In such uncertain times, her father had felt the need to run down the labor and delivery doctor to pay him twice the bribe he normally would have paid, if only to make sure the man didn't emigrate to Israel before his second born could come wailing out. For this act of paternal care and love, Mikhail Aleksandrovich Sverdlov was rewarded by the newly formed Russian Federation with almost three years of unpaid employment as a state hydroelectric engineer. By the time he had come to accept that there'd be no future for him in his area of training—and that if he had been smart, he would have studied English so he could have earned a few dollars working as an interpreter for all of the missionaries and documentary filmmakers coming through—he was making an appeal to an old friend from Komsomol, a man who'd been better prepared for the emergence of bandit capitalism. It was a simple transaction: at the cost of his pride, he secured a small loan to open a modest tire shop (before he even owned a car!). The venture proved profitable. Almost as quickly as Leningrad became St. Petersburg, his business grew large enough for him to buy a four-room apartment and rent out the two-room *Khrushchyovka* he'd been given as a parting gift from the final caretakers of the failed Communist state.

But the success he experienced in the mid-nineties, like everything else, soon passed. First the collapse of the ruble took away much of his fortune, and then a German tire chain arrived to cut into his profit margin and force him out of business entirely. By this point, my wife Dasha was already a student at the local polytechnic institute. She had known his successes as much as his failures. But Luba, then only nine, was far more impressionable. She had heard people speak of her father's former athletic prowess. She knew his time in the 200-meter breaststroke had once sent him traveling as far away as Poland and North Vietnam and even earned him a spot on the last national team to boycott the Olympic Games. But when she looked at the man before her, she didn't see a Master of Sport. She saw only someone who sat in front of the television every day, watching the same old Soviet movies over and over again.

Though my father-in-law rebounded in the coming years, the employment he enjoyed in the new millennium made Luba think no better of him. In fact, it only helped drive them further apart. It was his old friend from Komsomol who once again sent him a lifeline. He had by now gone from a small metals trader to a high-ranking official of an investment firm that was looking to broaden its interests in foreign utilities. They were building a dam in the Indian state of Andhra Pradesh, and he told my father-in-law he needed someone there he could trust. That is why Mikhail Aleksandrovich Sverdlov kissed his wife and children goodbye and like that became a hydroelectric engineer again, first in south India and then later in Panama. In between, he grew in his youngest daughter's eyes to nothing more significant than a smudged postmark on another letter sent to her from a distant and malarial land.

When he returned from Panama a few years before these events to accept a position working for the same state agency he'd once reluctantly stepped away from, Luba rebuffed his every effort to reconnect. How could she love him? She barely knew him. And even if she did, what would be the point? He didn't love her. He only questioned her. Questioned her decision to drop out of college, questioned her willingness to become "just" a beautician, and most of all questioned her choices in men. This goat? This is the man for you? She didn't want anything to do with him, nothing at all. That's why, when we told her we were planning to visit from the United States, she refused to greet us at his house, saying instead we'd have to arrange to get together later.

"I guess she meant Sweden," I told my wife after Luba's boyfriend had left.

Dasha didn't hear. She was cleaning up the table she'd set before the boyfriend had buzzed from the street and kept us from delivering the news we'd traveled here to share. Now her father remembered.

"You said you had something important to tell me?"

"It's nothing."

He grabbed her by the wrist as she reached for a plate of salted fish, but she pulled loose of him, then crossed her arms across her chest.

"She's always ruining things," she said. And then: "I'm having a baby. There. You're going to be a grandfather. Happy?"

A smile floated up onto my father-in-law's drunken face. "We should celebrate," he said.

Dasha lifted the empty bottle of *samogon* from the floor behind him. "How can we celebrate? We've already mourned."

"Well, there'll be plenty of time to celebrate later," I told them. Our suitcases were still by the door. We had ten more days before we were scheduled to leave.

"Then you won't mind if I see about something later tonight," her father said, and five minutes later he was gone.

I made it until seven o'clock that evening. Then jet lag fell upon me like an act of violence and I crawled into bed. I awoke an hour or two later, just long enough to hear the far-off sound of an old woman beating a rug clean in the courtyard ten stories below. When I came to again near midnight, it was to another sound that I heard: that of the front door opening and my father-in-law loudly coming in.

Leaving Dasha sleeping beside me, I went out into the front foyer as he was making a sport of hanging his summer jacket in the wardrobe. After finding his house shoes, he noticed my presence and insisted I follow him into the kitchen for a drink. We sat at the small table pushed up against the wall, and I accepted a rocks glass with three fingers of American whiskey (bought special for my visit, he said). Only after he had poured it did I realize I was drinking alone. He drank from a bottle of Narzan.

"I'm already up to here," he said, holding a hand a few inches above his forehead. "Drink," he instructed. "You're going to be a father. We must celebrate to mark the occasion."

By the time Dasha had come in to inspect the contents of the fridge, I was onto my second glass and had learned that my father-in-law had spent the last few hours with his old friend from Komsomol. He had hoped his connections in the government could bring this drama with his daughter to a swift end. But if Luba was already in Sweden, she'd make her case for refugee status to a low-level bureaucrat in Stockholm, not a career diplomat who might have passed through Russia and learned a thing or two about reciprocity in the process. Were they to forcibly repatriate her for speaking such lies? my father-in-law's old friend had asked. Should he have her delivered to Leningradsky Station in a sealed railway car?

"It would embarrass him to even ask," my father-in-law said, "so instead we drank."

My wife sat down beside me with a glass of kefir. "Let her go," she said. "There's nothing you can do. Either they listen to her madness and allow her to stay, or she comes back knowing for once she's a fool."

Dasha was just like her father. Cut in front of her in line at the store, or fail to yield to her car on the road, and she'd shake her finger in your face and call you a goat, maybe even spit on the ground, she'd be so upset. But if an entire system of government failed or the ruble collapsed, taking with it your entire life savings, she'd simply shrug her shoulders. She'd simply look at you as if you were showing her a child's dead goldfish. What do you want me to do? her look would say. Just flush it. They die. Let it go.

But there was one thing she couldn't see, and her father was happy to point it out to her as he affably waved a finger back and forth between them. "You don't know how it changes you. You sit there pregnant and still you don't know. I'm her father," he announced. "She's my daughter. I can't wash my hands of this." Then, half-standing from his chair, he reached into his back pocket and dropped three train tickets onto the table. "We'll go together."

Dasha fanned out the tickets and found the one printed in her name. "I'm not going to Sweden." Then: "How'd you even buy these?"

"Your passports are safe." He pointed to the front hall. "In my jacket."

She looked at him with a mixture of anger and disbelief.

"Don't look at me like that. I'm no thief, I'm your father." He continued to me now, saying we'd leave by train to Helsinki, then take the ferry from there. "Consider it a holiday. A holiday within a holiday. I'll pay for everything."

"On your state salary?" my wife asked. Since returning from Panama, the job there not yet even half done, his salary had been cut in half, if not further reduced, I knew.

"I don't have a mortgage like you," he told us. "I have money."

Dasha began speaking rapidly now—too rapidly for me to keep up with her Russian. Her point was clear, though: she didn't want to go, in fact she couldn't. She was four months pregnant, and she wasn't about to bounce across the Baltic Sea on a ferry, sixteen hours there and back, when already she'd celebrated her return to Mother Russia by vomiting into an air sickness bag on the runway at Pulkovo Airport.

My father-in-law sat through her entire speech like a man trying to hold his ground on a cheap folding chair in a wind tunnel. Then, pursing his lips and nodding, he tossed one hand high over his shoulder and said, "*Ladno*." Fine. "And you?" He looked directly at me, but I wasn't given any time to answer. Dasha spoke on my behalf: I would go, she told him, but only to keep him out of trouble. "You can teach him everything you know about fatherhood," she said. "I have my girlfriends to see. Just don't be more than a few days. I expect *shashlik* at the *dacha* before we leave."

Less than thirty-six hours later, after riding by train to Helsinki and then taking a ferry to Stockholm from there, we arrived in Sweden and my father-in-law revealed to me the first phase of his plan. Like a conquering general ready to claim victory as soon as he had stepped foot on foreign soil, he dialed his daughter's number from the ramp slanting down from the boat. I suppose he believed everything would be better, that Luba would return to Russia with us and their relationship would once again be strong, if only she could see how far he had come.

She didn't even pick up. My father-in-law stood there, his ear practically swallowing that tiny phone of his, as a vast crowd of passengers moved down around him onto dry land and off toward the entrance to the metro station.

By the time we were seated and hurtling toward the city center, he had recovered from this disappointment by developing plans that he described to me with such confidence and certainty that I dared not express any doubts. We would look for her at the Migration Bureau. She had been here only a few days, time enough to have registered for asylum perhaps, but not yet receive an interview. No doubt she would have to return to the Bureau to collect her LMA card, which granted her access to inexpensive health care and gave her the right to remain in the country until her case could be heard.

"It's all online," he told me, when I asked how he knew all of this. "How do you think immigrants go shopping for countries?"

At the Central Station, we transferred to the Blue Line and continued toward Sundyberg, from which it was just a short walk to the offices of the Migration Bureau. When we reached it, we discovered a grey, five-story building, encased in long strips of tin, that seemed to have been given the task of denying the stereotype of sleek Swedish design. It was also the wrong place. When I asked someone in the lobby where applications for asylum were accepted, I was told we needed the Solna office—a good three kilometers away, back in the direction we'd come from.

"You should have taken the commuter train, not the metro. Look for the building from the station. It's green-grey, and very ugly."

It was almost one o'clock by the time we got there—a smaller building this time, the waiting room of which was full of Somali men and women in hijabs and small Asian children running away from the outreached hands of their mothers. It could have been any DMV office I'd ever visited.

I approached a young woman at the registration desk who had dazzling white teeth and a long ponytail of whitish-blonde hair. Before I could reach her, though, my father-in-law had stepped in front of me and begun reading from a slip of crumpled paper he'd apparently secretly written on at some time during the night.

"I am looking for daughter," he said in his slow, deliberate English. "She is Russian. I must talk. I am not dangerous man."

Even if the suggestion of danger had been invoked only so it could be denied, the clerk, visibly alarmed, turned round in her seat and started speaking quickly in Swedish to what I assume was her supervisor. This man appeared from behind a wall of cubicles, wearing a baby blue knit tie, square at the bottom. He set his thin brown mustache into a straight line and spoke sternly to us through the wall of plexiglass, as if no one had ever told him he stood no more than five foot six and weighed not even a hundred and forty pounds. "This is not allowed," he said in his singsong Swedish-English. "You cannot intimidate refugees here."

My father-in-law looked to me, not sure how they had failed to understand the purity of his intentions. "What?" he said in Russian.

The Swedish man continued more loudly, telling us "these people" were wards of the Swedish government, and as such granted full protection.

"Hey, we're not trying to start a war here," I put in. "He just wants to speak to his daughter. I'm an American," I told him, inexplicably, helplessly, and ultimately for no good reason whatsoever.

The Swede took this as a challenge to his authority and spoke briefly of the wars in Iraq and Syria–"and God knows where else"–and how "your foreign policy of aggression and greed" had driven so many people here in the first place. "You are like a nation of cooks who refuse to clean up the kitchen afterward," he said, and the whole time the blonde at the front desk looked up at him as if he were rescuing children from a burning building. I wanted to kick them both in the knee. My father-in-law, meanwhile, oblivious to our rapid exchange in English, resettled into his Russian ways, saying first simply in English and then more loudly in Russian that his daughter—"Lubov Mikhailovna Sverdlova"—was no Chechen rebel, that she'd only been to Chechnya once—when her mother returned to visit her parents not long after her birth—but even then she had never stepped foot outside of Grozny. "She stayed with a childhood friend of her mother! Her grandfather never even knew about me! My wife took that secret with to her to the grave! My daughter's a beautician," he said, "not a sniper—tell them!" he said now to me, though by this point the Swedish man had moved past a door the receptionist had buzzed him through and fallen in alongside a security guard.

"Go!" the man was saying, pointing dramatically to the exit. "You must go now! Go!"

There was a modern hotel overlooking Sundyberg Station, but when my father-in-law learned they wanted close to $200 a night for a room—and would charge us for two full nights unless we waited another two hours to check in—he cursed the clerk and his country and started back for the street, leaving me to quickly ask the woman at the front desk to point us in the direction of more modest accommodations. They were back by the Migration Bureau office we'd just left, and "really more of a hostel than a hotel," she said.

The clerk's directions proved imprecise. The first four people I stopped either didn't speak English or hadn't heard of our "hostel or hotel."

"It's not that I am cheap," my father-in-law explained, sensing that I was growing aggravated at the length of our walk. "But Luba is like water"—here he dropped his hand from his shoulder to his waist—"she always seeks out her own level. It will be better to look here."

We hiked up one hill and then another, the bottles of vodka we'd bought from the ferry's duty-free shop clinking together in my wheeled carry-on. When we approached a shirtless man pushing a lawn mower across a tiny patch of grass, I asked my same tired questions and he pointed us down the hill we'd just ascended, saying we'd see a sign that led to a path—"Yes, a dirt path"—that went up at a sharp angle through the forested hillside to the Sundyberg Hotel & Hostel.

"Hotel and hostel?" I said.

"Indeed," he told me.

Once we had glimpsed our destination, my father-in-law hurried out in front of me, swinging his man purse wildly at one side. I felt no need to rush. The place was decidedly more of a hostel than a hotel. In fact, the L-shaped complex of red, flat-roofed buildings looked decidedly more like a barracks than a Holiday Inn.

In front of one of the nine connected wooden shacks, a couple of Sudanese men were roasting skewered meat on a mini hibachi. Two rooms down from them, an Arab in an ankle-length white robe stood in his doorway, as if surveying all that he had lost in his peripatetic life. Even before we could be given a key—not a key card, but a key—I could feel the musty sheets of the narrow bed I'd sleep in and see the mildewed tile on the floor of the bathroom's shower and imagine the briefs and socks that my father-in-law, who had refused to pack a change of clothes, would soak, squeeze, and leave to dry in the rust-stained sink.

Inside the reception room, a young English woman, obviously led astray by an all-too-positive online review, stood arguing in front of us, telling the clerk at the front desk about a laptop that had been stolen from her room. The clerk was a Swede of fifty-some years with a vaguely fascist haircut. When he was ready for their conversation to be over, he shifted into Swedish and looked to us while raising his chin.

My father-in-law stepped forward, opening his man purse and pulling out a picture. "Have you seen her?" he asked. The clerk gave the picture a cursory look (the English woman was still there, clucking in disbelief) then shook his head and looked to me, as if having decided I was going to be the one to pay.

"Do you take American Express?" I asked.

That night, we drank one of the three bottles of duty-free vodka, though there was no ice machine down the hall, meaning we could only chill it in the cold water of the sink. It helped bring about the sort of conversation I'd hoped for the night of our crossing, though instead of speaking about his daughter, my father-in-law told me, in the pantomime-accented English he often used when he was drunk, how he'd left his good-paying job in Panama against his own will.

"I"—and here he raised an imaginary bottle to his mouth, "Glug-glug-glug, then"—he began steering an invisible car, reasonably well before his eyelids began to flutter. "Boom!" he said, smacking his hands together. "A tree. Car of company." He waved, flapping his fingers up and down. "Bye-bye, Mikhail. *Do svidanya.*"

Though the walls at the hotel were thin enough for us to hear arguments in two different languages, it was the sound of a text message that woke me shortly after midnight. My father-in-law somehow heard it, too. Snoring one moment, he popped up from his pillow the next as if he'd been released by a spring. His phone vibrated, aglow beside him. "Luba," he said, reading from the screen. "She wants to meet in the morning."

At the designated time, I followed my father-in-law up to the recessed doorway of the still-closed Migration Bureau building. I had no idea why she had asked to meet him there so early, and if my father-in-law knew, he'd refused to say. I stood alongside him like the baker in *The Godfather*, wondering how I could protect the ailing Don Corleone with nothing more lethal than my finger. A few minutes passed, and then a pale young woman in a dark head scarf appeared from behind a dumpster at the back of the building across the street. She waved timidly. Luba, I realized. And then my father-in-law was off.

I followed after him, but his strides were longer than mine and he was walking even more quickly than usual. When I reached the middle of the street, I no longer felt that I should even join them. They were moving toward each other as if accelerating into a collision.

"What's this?" he barked. "A head scarf? You're no more Chechen than George Bush!"

"Keep your voice down," she said, now battering his chest with her fists. "Is it not enough that you ruin my childhood? Now this too? It's my one chance at a decent life! Don't you understand? There's nothing for me in Russia!"

He said something to her then, but his Russian was both too fast and too complex for my ears. It didn't matter. It'd take a fool not to understand. She was crying, the tears battering my father-in-law harder than any of her blows had. He pulled her toward him and wrapped her up in his arms so violently I thought he might be squeezing the last air from her lungs. She wept, wildly and openly, as no American would, and tried to escape his hold. But he held her more tightly, turning his back to me while speaking into her ear.

When finally he let her go, she wasn't the one to run. He was, though only after they'd exchanged a few final words. When he reached me, he said he needed my help, then led me to the corner, where together we took up a position behind an electrical substation of some kind.

"What are we doing?" I asked.

"I am her father," he said, as if that were answer enough. Then we waited.

By 7:50, I had to ask again: "Mikhail Aleksandrovich, what are we doing?"

He shushed me, pointing off down the street. A man was coming from the direction of the train station—the Swede from yesterday, the one with the thin mustache and the square-bottomed tie (yellow today, not blue). Almost immediately after I had comprehended this, my father-in-law was racing toward him and then lifting the man off his feet and pushing him hard into the side of the Migration Bureau's building.

I ran after him, but stopped when I realized I couldn't possibly do anything. I have the body of an economics professor, which is in fact what I am, while my father-in-law, though at least forty pounds overweight, retains the long body of a once-exalted swimmer. I stood there on the sidewalk listening as he spoke words that were both guttural and harsh. Near the time I understood that I looked like an accomplice, he turned to me, saying I should come closer and translate from Russian into English.

"I am a Chechen warlord," he had me say, "and I came here to stop my most valuable sniper from leaving, because she is also my favorite wife."

I spoke these words as if channeling them from a distant planet, and because I didn't know the word for "sniper," my father-in-law had to set the Swede down and make a quick pantomiming action—one that terrified his hostage all the more.

"But I see now," I continued, when he had lifted the Swede up again, "I cannot control her, and my happiness depends on her happiness. Ignore what I said yesterday at your own risk. I am a very dangerous man."

My father-in-law released the Swede, then, asking if he understood. The Swede answered in his own language—a curse, I presume—and hurried into the building and locked the door behind him as we watched. It was like a spell had been cast, and now it was broken. Remembering my pregnant wife, I ran up the street as if to escape a Swedish jail. Then I stopped, realizing my father-in-law wasn't at my side. This isn't a story about immigration or Russia or the most favored nations of this world. This is a story about my last strong memory of those years before I became a father myself. Standing there in the middle of the road as a car went honking by, I saw him walking once more around that dumpster, a father looking again for his daughter, unable to believe she was gone.

At the Tejas Rodeo

Bulverde, Texas

I show up early so as not to miss the gunshot
that starts the show and to be at the chain-
link fence up front, see the chaos
of the bleachers filling up, the riders saddling,
the cowboys readying the bull, driving the bull
to be crazed enough to jump, to be lassoed.
And they line horses up for good reason,
and I pick the one with the loneliest name,
Last Gleaming, as my favorite. A patch over
his blind left eye and a birthmark
the size of the star on the Texas flag.

All please rise comes over the speakers
and the woman standing in the dirt
starts to sing the National Anthem.
Everything she wears is leather.
I smell that smell of leather, I could
smell that smell forever.
I put my hand over my heart. Or, shoot,
is that the Pledge of Allegiance?
Either way I hold my hand to my heart.

Joint Readiness

We didn't see any action. The squad training exercise was bullshit. Opposition Forces—bands of bored civilians playing our enemy—probably forgot about us and was somewhere getting hammered. Instead, we fought the scorching hot sun. Chugged water like beer. Apologized to our rifles for not firing them. Back at the barracks Freck was pissed. Pissed he hadn't seen anything. He wanted to finally see something. See something blow up. Hill said, "Watch this." He attacked a pimple on his forehead. Right in the middle. Pulsing a brilliant red like a bull's-eye. We watched him execute one last squeeze to the bulging whitehead. It blew up on his greasy skin. He slid on his sunglasses, fell back on his cot, and was dead asleep in seconds.

We got hungry. But we didn't want MREs. They stopped up our insides.

Freck, playing Madden on his PSP, said, "Snack run?"

Sgt. Russell rolled his eyes and said, "Fuck it."

There was a 7-Eleven just outside the training area. So that was our mission, our objective. Russell, Freck, and me rallied around the trailer taking orders and collecting cash, $60 to be exact. Nobody trusted us with their debit and credit cards. I wouldn't have trusted us either.

We were ordered to buy all kinds of chips, pain pills, hot dogs, sodas, dental floss, an egg salad sandwich, porn or anything-close-to-porn magazines, Vaseline, Skittles, and whatever other random-ass shit that could nourish our bodies. Freck scribbled all of it down. We saddled up in the Humvee with the list and the sixty bucks. Sergeant Russell drove. I rode shotgun. Freck—recently re-demoted—sat in the back. We were on a mission to take the 7-Eleven. Our M4s stood between our legs. Muzzles pointing toward hell.

Russell carefully navigated us through the MP checkpoint, winding past cement barriers. A couple left turns and a right and we were on the main road. The Humvee rolled smoothly onto the asphalt, leaving the sand and dirt behind us.

It was like driving to another world, another dimension. Teleporting from a fake war zone—soldiers strapped with fully loaded rifles, OPFOR, barracks trailers, ammo tents, makeshift TOCs—into a suburbia of trees towering over huge two-story houses with paved driveways. Kids playing with dogs and waving at us from front yards. People washing and waxing their trucks and SUVs. We flew by some brand-new barracks that resembled a five-star hotel. Russell gawked at some new NCO club with a rooftop bar. He nearly ran off the road. Freck partially unzipped his window to let the humid air circulate. I unzipped mine all the way. Let the flap hang. There's something about fresh air. I propped my arm on the sill, inviting the hands of the wind to caress my face.

Freck unfolded the list and started reading out all this random shit. He read so fast he could have been speaking in tongues. When he was done, he started going back over it, asking questions: "What flavor Cheetos did Crowe say, hot or regular? What flavor taquitos does Hill like?"

"If they didn't give a flavor, fuck 'em," Russell said. He booted the gas and the list flew from Fleck's fingers. I snatched it before it got sucked out my window. It felt like I had saved some sacred text from antiquity. I read it carefully, trying to memorize who wanted what. When I got to Wilkins, I stopped.

"Wilkins doesn't need any more damn Twinkies. He eats one more and homeboy's going to blow up. Cream filling and pieces of golden cake hitting us like shrapnel."

Freck laughed, beating on the empty seat beside him.

But Russell didn't respond. His wife was big, I'd forgotten—a single one of her thighs was around the size of Russell's torso—and he was small, a bone-thin, wiry dude. Maybe Russell didn't laugh at my Twinkie joke because he was personally offended; I didn't mean anything by it. Or maybe it was because I made a joke about bombs and shrapnel. But none of us had been to war yet. We hadn't seen anything like that. So it was probably because of his big, lovely wife.

Russell, like me and Freck, was deploying for the first time. Crazy to think a sergeant had never deployed. All three of us in the Humvee were only a few months away from our first tour. And maybe our only one.

"Who's got the money?" Freck yelled over the groaning air.

"Zip your fucking window," Russell said. "Can't hear you."

"Who the hell's got the money?" Freck yelled back.

"Me," Russell screamed. "And I ain't having no replay of Walmart, ya hear?"

"Fuck you." Freck scolded Sgt. Russell's reflection in the rearview. "Why you gotta bring that shit up?"

"Sergeant," Russell said.

"Huh?"

I saw Russell's smirk. "Fuck you, Sergeant," he said.

Freck unzipped his plastic window all the way. The little clump of hair on top of his head fell back in retreat.

Me and Freck were close before he got arrested for stealing cough medicine from the Walmart up the road from our post. We used to hit the bars together. Played Madden on his Xbox. Flirted with girls at local high school football games. But when the police caught him with those bottles of Robitussin and NyQuil, all of that stopped. Later, he spray-painted "I hate the Army" on a brick wall of the barracks. I thought he was done. Thought he'd be kicked out of the Army for sure. But Platoon Sergeant saved his pale ass, saying it was the stress of deployment weighing on him. So Freck avoided discharge a second time. By the skin of his teeth, as my Moms would say.

In the rearview I stared at the reflection of the bare Velcro in the middle of Freck's ACU top, where his rank patch used to be. Don't do stupid shit, as my Moms would say.

Vehicles in the lot at 7-Eleven consisted of old pickup trucks, SUVs, vans driven by Army wives, and one white BMW M6. I was surprised we were the only Humvee. I figured there'd be more soldiers trying to escape.

"In and out," Russell said.

I held the door open for a tatted-up brunette whose hair swayed as she passed. She thanked me. She had a nose ring hooked in one nostril. Probably the wife of some officer. I covered her six, followed her inside. She smelled like a gun range full of gardenias.

"Guess I ain't pretty enough for you to hold the door for me?" Freck said.

I watched as the woman strutted over to the coffee counter. Then I looked at Freck, eyeing him from his ugly boots to his balding head. "Nope," I said.

Russell started calling out items off the list.

Me and Freck tore through the aisles of that 7-Eleven dodging stunned parents and wide-eyed kids. Scooping up bottles of pills, snatching up chip bags mostly filled with air, candy, impulse-buy-shit at the register, stuff no one asked for: buy-one-get-one-free cookies, gum, mints, dry pizza from a heated cage. I grabbed an apple—because a brotha gotta have a balanced diet. We had everything except the Twizzlers, and I couldn't believe my eyes when Freck robbed the last pack out of some kid's hand. I thought he'd break into tears. Start screaming. But when Freck bent down and whispered in his ear, the kid let it go and took off.

At the register, I said to him, "What the fuck was that?"

"Told him a life lesson," Freck replied. "I told him, 'Snitches get stitches.'"

Good thing Russell didn't hear it. We would already be in push-up position, kissing filthy tiles. Russell was feeling himself that day, walking with his bird chest out. Wanting everybody to call him Sergeant, even the clerk at the register.

"My mistake," the clerk said, bagging up all our junk. "That'll be $39.76, Sergeant."

Russell smirked at us as he paid the woman $40, depositing the face of Andrew Jackson into his uniform's breast pocket. Me and Freck took up the bursting bags. Russell made a big show of opening the door for us, then let it close on the woman with the nose piercing. The door hit her coffee and she spilled some on her dress.

When we got outside I watched a man walk over from the Hardee's across the street. He was checking out our Humvee. The dude was tan and bald, dressed in a dingy Harley-Davidson tee. Jeans ripped at the knees and falling apart at the cuffs above a tattered pair of grey no-brand sneakers. One of the soles was separated from the rest of the shoe. A flapping jaw.

"You boys must be gettin' ready to head on out." His lips formed a crusty smile.

"Yep. Afghanistan," Russell replied, making for the Humvee's driver's side.

"I was in Desert Storm myself. You boys infantry? I'm infantry." The old man pulled a cigarette from his pocket. The thing sat limp between his chapped lips.

"We're some stone-cold killers," Freck said.

Russell shot Freck a look, shook his head.

"Killers? You killed yet?" The old man lit his cigarette. "All that junk food is killers."

His laugh was guttural, deep, like phlegm was held hostage in his throat.

"I can tell y'all ain't no killers. You ain't gots that look." He blew smoke at my face.

"What look?" Freck said.

"You know. That look. The one that can see through a man. Past all his bullshit. Into his soul." He took a long pull from his cigarette. The small cherry at the end burned into a red worm of ash. "This look." He turned to face me, widening his blue eyes so the meaty white bulged out.

For some reason, this crazy motherfucker chose me for his target practice. So I put on my black-dude-from-the-hood-don't-fuck-with-me face. Tilting my head up, clenching my jaw. Tightening my lips, squinting. It worked on white kids back home, but this dude kept right on staring. Didn't even blink. I held my gaze on those icy blue irises and the little red veins closing in from all around. Eyeballs, that's all I saw. Not a glimmer of soul or life. He looked at me like I wasn't even there. I blinked. Blinked again. Figured those eyes had seen some things that shouldn't have been seen. I knew that one day soon I would see the same type of shit. And later I might see through people too.

"See?" He choked on his laughter.

"Come on," Russell said, signaling with his head. "Dude's crazy."

Cigarette smoke crept from the man's nostrils. "I'll show you crazy."

Freck chuckled. "OK, show us."

The man bent down to put his cigarette on the curb near the back of the Humvee and started rolling up one of his jeans legs. As he kept going, I noticed the sock, white and clean and bright. Before I had a chance to realize my mistake, I was already doubled over with a hand at my mouth.

"Fuck. Holy shit."

"See," he said, moving the leg close to my face. "That's crazy."

It was like something big had taken a bite out of it. No calf muscle. The leg's whole back was missing. The skin that remained was scarred and smooth, a trace of melted flesh. Whalebone white. He rolled the pant leg up past his big knee. The proportions were all wrong. Like a head on a stake.

"Let's get the fuck outta here," Russell said. He hustled over to the driver's side and switched on the engine. Me and Freck opened our doors and jumped in.

The old man limped over, rested an arm on my window, leaning in close.

"What?" Russell said. "We're headin' back."

Trapped phlegm gurgled in his throat. "You boys got anythin' to spare for an old soldier?"

"No," Sgt. Russell said, jerking the lever to Drive.

"Come on, Russ," I said. "Sergeant. Give him something."

Freck started rummaging around in one of the bags of junk food.

"I ain't all that hungry," the man said. "Just ate." He nodded toward the Hardee's and turned back to Russell and me.

"Sergeant, just help the guy out." I was feeling sorry about his half-blown-off shin, but more than anything I was feeling like I wanted to get the fuck out of this place.

"Yeah, Sergeant, help a fella soldier," the man said. A wave of hot cigarette breath crashed into my face. The man had a yellow-plagued smile. Looked like dirty raw gold in his mouth.

"Jesus fucking Christ." Russell undid the Velcro of his breast pocket and slid out the twenty.

The man's bony fingers gripped the bill's edge. Every fingernail was caked in black dirt.

"I 'preciate ya, Sarge," the man said. "You killers watch ya step over there."

As we sped off, I watched him in the side mirror. He stuffed the twenty in his pocket then picked up his cigarette off the curb. Stuck it back between his lips. He fixed his pants leg before limping over to another Humvee that had just rolled up.

No one said shit on the drive back. Russell thumbed the cheap onyx wedding band that was too big for his scrawny finger. Freck sat still in the back seat, peering out the window, probably strategizing ways to get promoted. The plastic bags on the seat next to him made a loud ticking noise from the wind.

I considered the long spine of the road in front of us. Scanned the sides of the narrow, two-lane pavement. What in the hell happened to homie with the fucked-up leg? How'd he end up begging for money like that? How can someone who was nearly blown to pieces resort to pleading for cash? I heard the voice in my head from the training video we'd watched a few days before. About the Taliban and their IED attacks, staging roadside bombs under pieces of trash, in shrubbery, in animal carcasses. If you see disturbed earth, heaps of trash, new bushes, rocks, dead dogs or livestock, be alert. Anything out of the ordinary. Be the fuck alert. The last part of the video messed everybody up. An up-armored Humvee drove through a barren valley when the earth burst from below. Shit happened so fast I would've missed it if I'd blinked. Pieces of the truck were in the clouds before the audio's blast.

Russell was still fingering his wedding band and started drifting. The Humvee's tires clipped the grass. We veered, flirting with the edge. Russell booted the gas and the plastic bags ticked louder. There was a man-made ditch adjacent to the road with trash scattered everywhere. I was scanning every inch. Feeling the bones in my legs.

When we entered the trailer, me and Freck pulled the mags, pills, snacks, treats, and drinks from the plastic bags. I handed Branch his Funyuns, Hill his taquitos, Crowe his Hot Cheetos, Lloyd his Skittles. Tossed Wilkins his Twinkies—he ripped them open and stuffed one in his mouth. I caught Russell's gaze in my periphery as Wilkins wolfed it down. He wasn't going to blow. I knew that. And after all that shit with the old man, the joke wasn't funny anymore.

Somebody asked Russell, "Where the hell's our change?"

He told the platoon about the man and the fucked-up leg.

But I wasn't listening. Lloyd had ripped his bag in half. Skittles rained down on the linoleum, rattling around and scattering. Like a damn rainbow had detonated. That clumsy motherfucker shouted at us to freeze, worried somebody might crush a Skittle under their boot. But nobody gave a shit. Homeboy dove onto the floor, scrambling to recover every last one. He yelled at us to watch where the hell we were stepping.

Photo by Ben Katarzynski

Daily Affirvotions

Those pains in your chest aren't a heart attack, it's that bra you've been wearing since high school.

No, you're not fat, your friend's just built like a runway model.

That face you glimpsed in the storefront window, don't worry, it wasn't yours (and of course they sell those jeans in your size).

You look old in that picture only because you're holding a newborn. But no, no worries, that baby's not yours.

You're not pregnant for at least five different reasons. And certainly not, no, not one of them is menopause.

That's just a pimple, a hangnail, an ordinary mole.

Did you forget you left your place a mess? No, you haven't been burglarized.

No one has used your credit card in El Paso; no one's charged a slushy, a Slim Jim, and 50 cartons of Winstons.

Yes, you spellchecked that message, changed shits to shirts before clicking send. And that letter, yes, it had plenty of postage; the receiver has just chosen not to reply.

Your car is in park, parking brake on. It has not rolled through the garage door, down the driveway, and out into the quiet street. No, your headlights aren't on.

Those are white hydrangeas, not doctors staked in the bushes. No, that's a unicorn, not a police car.

Relax, no one's looking at you. That fine young gentleman's not staring, he sees right through, to the unicorn standing behind you,

and as for God, as for God you're good, God doesn't see you either.

The Ghost Apple

Friday night: two whole days stretched ahead, alone with him, in the house.

She sat in the car, in the black cold of January, staring at the back door. A fizzy feeling rose in her chest like carbonation, as if she were just starting to turn the cap. It might be fine, she thought, it might not overflow. It all depended on what mood he was in. And there was no way to tell: she had to turn the cap. She had to turn the door knob…

The porch light switched on.

Just leave. Back the car out and go. She could do that if it was her husband who made her scared to come home after work. *But what if it's your son?* she wondered. *What do you do then?*

He peered out from behind the kitchen curtains.

Mothers aren't supposed to ask that kind of question.

"Mama," he cried happily, hugging her as she pushed open the door. "What took you so long?"

But Saturday was a good day. After days of freezing rain, the sun came out and the weariness of winter was transformed. All the branches were covered in ice. Together, they walked down the old railway bed, the center aisle of a glistening world.

He held her hand. She told him the legend of the fugitives who escaped from the state penitentiary almost a hundred years ago, a town legend she had grown up with as a girl.

At the covered bridge, she said, "They stole a car, and this is the very spot where they ran out of gas."

His brown eyes widened under his knit cap.

"And then the local men formed posses and went out with their rifles. All the women and children huddled in the houses with the doors locked."

"For real?"

"Yup. It was two days before a farmer finally found them."

His eyes locked on something in the distance. "I know where the fugitives could hide and never be found."

And then he was gone, racing up the hill toward the old, overgrown orchard. She struggled to catch up with him, breaking through the crusty snow with her boots.

Up ahead, he stopped dead in his tracks. Fear rushed through her. Was it an animal? "Mama, look."

When she finally caught up to him, he pointed to the limb of an apple tree. There it was: a hollow, apple-shaped sphere of ice, hanging delicately from a branch, beckoning to be picked. A ghost apple, they called them, created when ice freezes around the apple and then temperatures warm enough for the mushy flesh to fall out, leaving behind a perfect replica. She had heard about them before but had never seen one.

Neither said a word. It felt wrong to speak. Like being in a cathedral or a museum. Somehow, instinctively, he knew this, even at nine years old.

He was Adam, standing in the arctic Garden of Eden. The long seconds before the choice.

When they got back, she built a fire to warm their toes. He was excited to tell her all about his new ideas for a book about the fugitives. In his book, they would never be captured; they would make a secret town, high up in the hills of Vermont.

He was happiest when he was creating, whether with his hands or designing with ideas in his mind. It didn't matter if they ever came to be. She found herself starting to get excited too, offering suggestions, making plans. He leaned his body against her shoulder. She allowed herself to feel the warmth, the solidness, the contact. She counted in her head, almost up to twelve, until he shifted away.

"Do you want to roast marshmallows in the fireplace? Like we used to?" She was feeling playful. An ease had set in.

While she was in the kitchen, fishing for the skewers with the wooden handles, she heard a groan of frustration, followed by the sound of something shattering on the wooden floor.

"It won't work!"

When she got back to the living room, he had already stormed up the stairs.

The Lego spaceship. It had taken two days to build. Five hundred eighty-six pieces on the floor, flung like colored constellations across the sky.

She heard him upstairs in his bedroom, kicking the wall, screaming.

It was her fault, her husband insinuated later that night when he got back and examined the foot-shaped crater in the plaster. She never should have left the spaceship on the dining room table.

The therapist called it the "red zone" when he was past the point of return. She was not supposed to give him any attention then. *Refuse to give energy to the negative behaviors.* She recited this quote in her mind to strengthen her resolve. *I absolutely refuse to give energy to the negative behaviors.* She repeated it as he tore down posters in his room, threw his iPad. Once, he broke a pane of glass.

They had tried everything that parents try. They had threatened consequences and they had even followed through: time-outs, no screens. She had tried talking to him, using a soothing and validating tone. They read books about emotions, came up with cute little drawings to remind him of his coping strategies and posted them in conspicuous places around the house.

Briefly, when he was four, in total exasperation, she'd asked her husband, Brian, to spank him. She remembered bathing him and seeing the bruises on his skinny little bum. Brian cried in bed that night. She didn't ask any questions, and they never spanked him again.

Nine years they had tried, if you included the years of his colicky infancy. They kept going with the point charts, long after he no longer cared.

And here they were. A gray February afternoon.

"I don't want a point," he screamed. "I want a hug!"

He was lying on the hallway floor, writhing as if in pain.

She felt her body wanting to respond, wanting to swoop in, as parents do with their hurting child. But the words echoed. *Refuse to give energy to the negative behaviors.*

So instead she walked from room to room, putting away the laundry, tidying up the mess. He crawled after her, whining and making animal noises. At one point, she locked herself in the bathroom. She sat on the toilet, clutching her phone, as the carbonation swelled in her chest. She thought of texting Brian, but there was nothing he could do to help her. She was alone, anxiety spilling over her sides.

Minutes passed. Finally, she heard soft moans coming from downstairs and thought perhaps the meltdown was subsiding. She opened the door and stepped hesitantly down the stairs. He had crawled into his box fort. The next time he whimpered, "I want a hug," she allowed herself to respond. She crouched down to peer into the fort. Just as she was reaching out, he yelled, "I hate you! Get away!"

He kicked at the cardboard, denting it until it toppled over on himself. As she turned to walk away, he surged out and grabbed her shirt, pleading, "Mama, please don't go, please don't leave me."

She tried to pry him off, but his grip was strong. His eyes craved her with animal hunger, tears streaming down his face. "Don't go!"

Refuse to give energy to the negative behaviors.

She kept walking, dragging his weight behind her, until finally he let go and fell to the floor. He thrashed his body then, the way a drowning man flails, as he reached for objects to throw. A Nerf gun splintered against the hutch. A Rubik's cube gouged plaster from the wall.

She had to leave. She had no choice. Her very presence was the energy that seemed to make him worse.

The sun was setting as she drove to the top of the mountain road. Her plan was to quickly turn around at the trailhead; she didn't want him to think she wasn't returning. But, as she crested the hill, the ruddy ball dropped, plunk, down into the pocket behind the ridge, more beautiful because it was blurred through her tears. If she had been one minute later, she would have missed it.

The perfect moment. She had to stop and watch.

She was gone no more than fifteen, twenty minutes at most. When she returned, he was standing on the porch in his Minecraft pajamas, his arms outstretched, holding a baking tin. As she climbed the steps, he said, "I'm sorry, Mama. I made you an apology salad." It was arugula mixed with hacked-up pieces of strawberry. They had locked up the knives long ago, so he'd used a fork to cut the strawberries.

"Thank you," she said. She knew the tantrum was over.

At the dinner table, he watched her closely as he ate his chicken nuggets. His eyes arched, full of light, when she took a bite of salad. "You like it?" Somehow, he had managed to get a blob of ketchup in his eyebrow.

And in that moment, the grit of unwashed salad in her teeth, she was overcome by a powerful urge: she wanted to die so that this freckled boy with ketchup in his eyebrow could be well.

It made no sense. It wasn't an option that existed in this world, but she wanted desperately, right now, this instant, to extinguish her own life for his. And as quickly as the urge came, it passed, and she was shrouded in sadness, for she knew she loved this boy more than she loved her husband. More than any child they could ever conceive.

The next morning, she told her husband to go ahead with the vasectomy. She was approaching forty now, so they had to decide. They had waited nearly ten years, hoping he would get better.

Brian crawled into bed around five a.m. after working a double.

She turned over in bed to face him and said, very reasonably, very calmly, "So I've been thinking…"

He yawned, "Yeah?"

He was used to these early morning musings. It was often the only time they had to talk. They had to work opposite hours now because they couldn't leave their son with anyone else, couldn't send him to after-school care.

"We can't bring another child into the world, not the way he is. We can barely take care of him."

She knew Brian was relieved, though she noticed that he was careful not to show it too much. He clutched her hand on top of the blanket.

"I'm sorry," he said.

She didn't tell him the real reason—that she would never be able to love another child the way she loved this one. That there is a different level of love that comes when you must fight for someone to live. She didn't expect him to understand. He was snoring soon anyway.

When she heard someone was pregnant, there was a pang. It passed quickly, but it was there.

Her "friends" on Facebook posted ultrasound photos like blank slates, Rorschach ink-blots to project their dreams. They posted pictures of their blank-faced babies, snuggling in sleep. As she scrolled, a crease formed in the corner of her mouth like a tiny spade. For she knew what they did not—that at the point of conception, the die has been cast, the cards have been dealt.

Yes, the jaded smile hid her envy. But it was not a real child she desired. She was envious of the unknown card, the card face-down, and that beautiful blind courage one needs to flip it over. She wanted to go back to when she was just like them, before she knew, when there was just possibility. She could be excited then; she could dream.

He had labels now. Five different diagnoses, stuck on him at different times by different professionals. Anxiety. ADHD. Bipolar Disorder. Autism. Oppositional Defiant Disorder. When she had first brought him to be evaluated at age five, she was so afraid of shame, so afraid they would tell her she was a bad parent. She was convinced they were all judging her from behind the safety of their clipboards. Every appointment felt like a job performance review; she recited all the strategies they had tried, all the books she had read.

After a while, she realized it wasn't her fault. She did what reasonably educated parents do. And it didn't work. Then she blamed herself for being so damn consistent, for not realizing sooner that he wasn't like other children. She shivered when she remembered putting him back on the "naughty step" when he was a toddler, the fits that lasted hours, sometimes so bad he threw up. Why had she persisted? Was she that determined to win?

Now, truthfully, as he neared his tenth birthday, she was past the fear of being ashamed. She was angry. Why couldn't people give her any definitive answers? After all the letters at the end of their names, after all their fancy schools, deep down, in her gut, she knew they didn't know.

Every month, they drove over an hour to Burlington. Dr. Adams was their third psychiatrist, recommended by those who had given up. They sat in geometric-patterned chairs, waiting for Dr. Adams' pretty, twenty-something-year-old nurse to call them in. Jill. How she hated Jill, with her tidy blonde bun and the big diamond on her finger.

"Hey, friends. Good to see you again."

Jill measured his height and weight. She murmured, as if it were some personal concern, "Hmm…still at fifty-nine pounds."

It was the stimulants. He hadn't grown in a year. She wanted to stab Jill.

"Can I touch it?" her son asked, looking at the mini lava lamp on Jill's desk. He was already reaching for it as he asked.

Jill read through the long list of medications, wincing when he shook the lamp.

Each difficult-to-pronounce medication name felt like a new affront to her motherhood. She wanted to scream: *You don't understand! I'm forced to flee my own house! Do you think I want to stunt my son's growth?* But she didn't scream. Instead, she corrected Jill's pronunciation and glared at the cheery sign on her desk: "One small positive thought in the morning can change your whole day." The sign was next to a picture of her tanned husband, probably some doctor at the hospital.

She was sure Jill blamed her. It was better that way—to keep the illusion of a mother's control. If it was her fault, Jill needn't worry when her own time came. Surely, she wouldn't make the same mistakes.

At least Dr. Adams was older, nearly her parents' age. He had seen too much to be cheery. She felt relaxed in his presence. It was the messy office and his gentle tone.

"Well," he said. "So tell me…" That's how every appointment began.

"He's the same." She hated to say it, like she was announcing defeat, not just for her, but for the doctor as well. "He—"

She heard noises behind her. Her son had gone straight to the bookcases as usual, looking for something to play with. Dr. Adams waved his hand, as if to dismiss her concern. "Go on."

So she told him about the Lego spaceship, the meltdown in the box fort. He listened.

She waited until her son was in the bathroom before she said, "I'm scared. He's going to go through puberty in a few years, become a teenager. I just worry, what if he isn't OK?"

She didn't say it, but she was thinking of violence. Of jail, even. She was thinking that soon he would be bigger than her.

At least Dr. Adams didn't patronize her. He shut his laptop and looked at her for a long moment. "It could go either way," he said with a sigh. "I've seen kids like him get better with age, as their executive functioning improves. Of course, if there is an underlying mood disorder, adolescence—"

Luckily, her son was coming in the door at that moment. The conversation was over, at least for now. She wasn't ready for it.

She was relieved when finally there was a new nurse. A pudgy older lady who made silly jokes. She didn't ask where the young nurse, Jill, had gone. Afraid of feeling the pang, smiling the spade, if the older woman said, "Maternity leave."

It was early spring when he was hospitalized for the first time. She was at work and the school couldn't reach her, so they called her husband. From what she pieced together later, some child had said something on the playground that set him off. Her son had fallen as he was running away, and then another child reached down to help him up, but he didn't understand, he felt under attack, and he lashed out defensively and hit the boy who was trying to help. Things like this had happened many times before. But this time was different because he ran away. They couldn't find him. This time he ran too fast.

When she got out of her meeting, she had ten missed calls. She called Brian first. "They can't find him," he said. He was breathless from walking the streets around the school. "But it's OK. They called the police. They have cruisers out. It'll be fine."

She was driving home, going eighty miles per hour on the highway, when it hit her. She called Brian back. "I know where he is. The old abandoned orchards behind the covered bridge. Check there. I know where he went."

By the time she got back to town, they had already found him and brought him back to the school. He was sitting at a table in the guidance counselor's office, an officer standing outside the door. They were waiting for the school district's psychologist to arrive. They wanted to evaluate him.

His boots were covered in mud, his brown corduroys were ripped at the knee, and he had scratches on his face from running through the woods. She saw a white bandage on one arm.

Brian explained that he had been missing for almost two hours. He had climbed one of the old apple trees. She imagined him in the tree, peeking out from behind the gnarled branches, a jungle boy. Wild and free. Of course, she was relieved he was safe. God had answered her frantic prayers. But now, looking at him from the doorway, she felt bad for him—caught, humiliated, a failed fugitive. His head was down; she could tell he had been crying. Someone had put a puzzle in front of him and he was blinking at it dumbly. He had always hated puzzles, no room for creativity.

She moved toward him and gave him a big hug, burying his scratched, freckled face in her hair. "Thank God you're safe, honey. Thank God you're safe." When she let him go, he didn't make eye contact.

"Can I watch YouTube on your phone?" he asked.

Once he was distracted, her husband whispered in her ear, as if it were some graphic, detestable detail, "He was singing when they found him."

"What was he singing?"

"What? What does it matter? He was singing."

"Sometimes he sings lullabies to calm himself down. It's one of his coping strategies," she said, thinking: *you'd know if you ever bothered to look at the list on the fridge.*

The school psychologist was with her son for almost an hour. He came out, careful to leave the door open, and sat with her and Brian in the secretary's office. All the teachers and students had left for the day.

After she heard the word "hospital," it was hard for her to focus on any other details. She tried to remain calm.

"He didn't mean any harm to the boy. He just gets like that when he feels under threat, when he's in the red zone. He's not in control of his body."

"It's not that," the psychologist said patiently. "It's that when I asked him if he wanted to hurt himself, he said he did. He says he doesn't want to be alive and—"

"Of course, he doesn't. Not right now, not when he's like this. But when we get him home, after he resets, and he can look at his Lego catalogues, and feel safe again—"

Brian cut her off. "Let him finish."

The psychologist continued. "He said he doesn't want to be alive, that he thinks everyone hates him, and when I asked him if he ever thinks of how he would hurt himself, he said he would jump off a bridge or he would shoot himself."

"Obviously, we don't have guns in the house." She was getting mad now. "We're not idiots. I lock up the knives, for Chrissake. I have to enter a combination every time I want to make dinner."

"You don't need to swear," Brian said.

"I mean," she said, managing to control her tone, "that we make sure that he can't act impulsively. We have alarms on all the doors, so we can hear if he goes out."

"He says you sometimes leave him alone."

"No—I—only for about ten minutes."

"The cuts on his arm are quite serious."

"Aren't they just scratches from climbing the tree?"

"They're deep. I had a chance to look under the bandages. They don't require stitches, but they don't look accidental to me. Looks like he may have gouged at himself with a stick. When I asked him if he scratched himself on purpose, he wouldn't answer me."

She could feel herself deflating. She was giving up. She looked at Brian. She was sinking, and her husband, strong and solid beside her, said nothing. He could have saved her, he could have said something. He could have reached for her hand to keep her from drowning.

"Also"—the psychologist took a sharp breath—"when I asked him why he ran away, he said that 'they' told him to. I asked who 'they' were and he said, 'the bad men.' I'm not sure if he is having auditory hallucinations. That's why, at this point, I think we should consider a hospitalization. Just short-term of course, and of course it's completely your decision. It would give them a chance to observe him, possibly make some medication changes."

He added hesitantly, "And it would give you a short break."

"He's never slept away from home, not even for a single night," she said quietly. All fight had gone out of her.

Brian was asking questions now about the details. Where would they go? What was the process like?

"He's never slept away from home," she said again, this time to herself. And more quietly still, almost a whisper, "He still wears a Pull-Up at night."

She was looking at her son in the next room. Sitting quietly, head bowed over her phone. He had no idea.

Her husband could have said something in his deep, firm voice. He could have said, "We're taking our son home." But he didn't. He wrote down the information and thanked the psychologist for his help.

The thought first occurred to her when she was getting coffee in the hospital cafeteria. Her son had been there two days then, and she had rented a hotel room nearby so she could visit him every day. Even so, she was sleep-deprived. She had slept five hours over the last two nights.

I'm going to have to learn to be happy, even if he isn't okay.

She flipped her head around to see if anyone had heard the thought. Irrational, totally. But it felt like something illegal, something taboo, had just flickered in her mind.

Annoyed, the girl behind the counter shifted her weight. She had a purple stripe in her hair. "I said, do you want cream in that?"

"No, no, just black."

She needed to learn how to be happy, even if he wasn't OK. Could she do that? Did people *do* that? The thought vanished as quickly as it had surfaced and she couldn't get it back again. At least not in any convincing way.

When it was time to leave his hospital room, she piled his stuffed animals around his shoulders. She reminded him that Dr. Woolly was there, the woolly mammoth he had since he was four.

"I'll be back first thing in the morning."

"Dr. Woolly is not afraid of hospitals," he said, sounding unsure.

"No, he's not. That's right. He was there when you woke up from your tonsil surgery. He's good at taking care of you when you're sick."

"Yeah."

She walked away. Down the corridor and toward the elevator. The only way she could hold back the tears was to visualize her own expressionless face, vacant, floating—lifeless as the drowned.

Back in her hotel room, she didn't turn on the TV or even the lights. She didn't order room service. She sat by a window that couldn't open, overlooking the parking lot, as the last light died in her lap. April in Vermont. Just a dirty, colorless time, left behind as winter receded.

What would make it worth it in the end? She asked herself this question as she waited for Brian's call, a call that seemed to come a little later with each passing evening. *What would make it worth it in the end? This pain of motherhood?*

The only word she could come up with was "OK." All of it would be worth it if he was "OK." What a dumb word, a word that meant nothing, a placeholder. One of the most frequently uttered words in the world. And yet, this one dumb little word captured her deepest, most cavernous longing as a mother.

"Just let him be OK, Lord. Just let him be OK."

The prayer came out in soundless heaves. Her body knew what this meant, but her mind did not. She hadn't prayed since she was a child. And now she prayed all the time, in the shower, in the car driving. Sometimes before she turned the corner into his hospital room.

What was she praying for?

In the end, she didn't need to be close to him. God knows she didn't need him to be successful, whatever that was. She didn't even need him to be especially happy. She just needed to know he was OK. And then she would be OK. She could rest.

After a week, he was finally discharged. She thought there was something different about him when they brought him home, a silence that wasn't good. She told Brian this while he was unloading the dishwasher. It was his night off and they had just called for takeout. They had plans to watch a movie. She knew they should have sex. It had been weeks.

She almost didn't say it, but then she did. "There's something not right with him."

"What do you mean? He's better, he's calmer. The new medication is working."

It was seven o'clock. Her son was upstairs in his bed, flipping through his Lego catalogues. He didn't fight her when she said it was time to go upstairs. He just went. All day long, he said how tired he was.

"No, I know—but I just—" She couldn't put her finger on it. Was it the new medication? Or was he mad at her? Punishing her for abandoning him? There was something different.

She tried again. "It's like, I offered to work on his fort with him outside this afternoon. It was beautiful out, but he didn't want to. So then I offered to build Legos with him. We did for a little while, but he lost interest, just wanted to be by himself. He barely talks to me anymore."

"Look, can't you just appreciate the fact that he's calmer? That he's not tearing apart the house every other second?"

"But he's not himself," she persisted.

"Exactly," he said. "He's better."

"Not that you would notice," she muttered. "You didn't play with him before anyway."

"Maybe because I'm at work sixty hours a week."

"Well, I guess it's fine if you'd rather have a zombie as a son. Easier for you that way." She regretted it even as it was coming out of her mouth.

He slammed down the glass he was holding and walked out of the kitchen. She heard the screen door slam and the car start.

"Fuck," she said under her breath.

She hoped he was just getting the takeout. Not that it mattered if he returned. The night was ruined now.

It was May before she dared to open the windows.

One afternoon, she made tea and chose a sunny spot on the couch next to the cat. The comforting sound of the dishwasher whirred behind her, the sound that meant her chores were done. And that's when she did it. She opened the window to let in the sound of the birds and the smell of the grass. She took a deep breath.

His body had adjusted to the medication now. He was still quieter than before, but he was starting to play again, starting to create. He wasn't tired all the time. And yet, she had been hopeful before.

She thought about what they would do if he was in a good mood when she picked him up from school. Maybe they could walk the woods, look for mythical creatures. He had been interested in that lately. And if he wasn't in a good mood? She would bring his tablet for the car just in case and would come armed with snacks. He was usually starving when she picked him up, wired and agitated, like a skinny needle vibrating on the line between yellow and red. She would be ready.

Here she was, sitting on the couch, a whole hour before she had to get him. And it was already there. That little bubbly feeling, rising up.

Tomorrow was his tenth birthday. She had invited over a dozen guests. She hadn't dared to host a party since he was three years old.

She pushed through the screen door with her hip, carrying a platter of hamburger rolls. The door banged loudly behind her and she paused, just momentarily to take in the feeling of the May sun on her skin. The heat wasn't strong enough yet to envelop her like the bear hug of summer. This sun was delicate; it was fickle. She had to choose to take it in. But there it was nonetheless, sharpening after the cloud passed, stenciling the edge of the shade on the lawn. And if she focused her listening just enough, behind the sounds of the distant highway and the laughter by the grill, there it was: the warbler's bubbly call. It made her think of champagne.

She left the platter of rolls by the grill and went back in. She found a bottle she had chilled in the wine fridge, just in case there was a special occasion. She was peeling off the foil when she saw them outside the window. Their backs were to her. Brian was leaning over him, helping him to set up the arrow, the red target pinned to a willow tree about twelve feet away.

It was a handmade bow and arrow set that Brian had found online. She didn't know he had ordered the set until she saw her son opening it that morning. At the time, she glared at Brian. "What?" he said. "The arrows have rubber tips. I had one when I was his age."

But now she froze, motionless, the bottle in her hand, watching them from the window. What if he missed the target? Would he scream?

She watched as her son pulled back his elbow. Brian held his arm steady. Ready. Aim.

The arrow whizzed and hit the bullseye. He hopped up and down and then looked at his dad. It was just a moment, a flicker of pride that passed in profile between them, and there was no way to tell which way the pride went, to designate from where it first originated. It was theirs.

She almost missed it.

Brian tousled his hair and the boy was off. He ran down the hill, wild and free, holding up the bow over his head in triumph as he ran.

She paused. Then she decided to take two glasses out of the cabinet.

Down on the lawn, Brian had set up some plastic chairs. He was alone, the other guests gathering by the food.

"You're drinking champagne?" he asked. "I thought it gave you hangovers."

She shrugged her shoulders and sat down beside him, pouring him a glass.

They watched their son running in zigzags with his bow, weaving in and out of the sun and shadows. His two cousins, only four and five years old, giggled as they chased after him. What if he fell and they tumbled over him?

She took a deep breath.

"Did I ever tell you about the ghost apple? The one we found this winter?"

"You told me. You found it in the orchard."

"But did I tell you what he said when I finally caught up with him?"

"No."

"Well, he was silent for a long time."

Brian took her hand then and smiled. "Yeah?"

"And then he looked at me, and he said, really serious, 'I think I just want to stay in this second, Mama. I don't want to find out if I pick it.' I thought of that just now. When I saw you helping him aim his bow."

She poured herself another glass. "The second when it can still go either way. That's where I have to live."

"You're gonna be sorry tomorrow," he chuckled. But as he said this, he reached out to tuck the hair behind her ear and wiped her tear with his knuckle.

"Maybe," she murmured.

They sat holding hands across the plastic chairs, watching their son. He was sprawled on the lawn now, rolling away from his cousins as they tried to tickle him. Grass stuck to his brown curls. He laughed and laughed as he rolled.

She closed her eyes to feel the sun before it went behind a cloud.

Tupelo, MS

Crop dusters have gone missing. Parachutes are missing. Storm clouds, missing. Every owl has gone missing. Entire foothills, missing. There are no dogwoods or foxes to miss them. Radio towers are missing. A historical archive has always been missing. Unmarked graves have not been missed. Have been missed to death. Downtown is missing, the hardware store where Elvis bought his first guitar. The songs he took from juke joints, missing. The songwriters are still missing. Original names for the dirt have been missing a long time. The namers have not been missed. Have been missed terribly. A gospel just went missing. A gospel took all the blood it needed for its metaphor to work. My lover went missing today. My lover went missing 15 years ago. When neighbors spoke to him, they spoke to someone else. Even now, they speak about someone else. I found his old letters, missing from the hat box. Then, my mother, gone with the letters, still blazing in her missing fireplace.

[Boy] Meets Them

You wouldn't want me now. Not like that.
　　　If you'd made it to 2020, instead of 2007,
　　　we'd compare jowl lines & say we don't *feel*
　　　almost 40 but the younger somehow look
　　　younger. I'd tell you that, last week,
　　　someone called me "sir" from behind
　　　& apologized when I turned around.
　　　I couldn't get them to believe I didn't mind.
　　　I really didn't. In 1996, when you wanted
　　　me, my long hair offered its youth
　　　to bleach & coiled heat. My makeup labor
　　　clocked twenty minutes for each eye.
　　　You had a type & it was me, hours after
　　　waking for school. I'd watched my mother
　　　do the same, leading with lacquer, frost,
　　　& shoulder pads. She didn't know,
　　　I didn't know, there were other ways—
　　　so many other ways—to wear a body.
　　　Back then, I catalogued your masculine
　　　markers as the rebellious exception.
　　　Something to be drawn to, not imitate.
　　　If you were here, I'd tell you that I now
　　　live in a swamp where nothing dies.
　　　The air two-thirds water & full
　　　of microbial grandparents. There's no
　　　room, here, for polyester or bracelets
　　　or hair. Or, the swamp gave permission

to shed it all, escape into minimalism. My
first name is now one letter. Under it I grow
like a plant that finally can see the sky.
In front of mirrors, I relax under a new
uniform—a shirt buttoned to the neck, flats,
a small watch. I think of you after graduation,
having finally cut your hair above the ears.
Did you notice a lightness, is what I'd say
if you were here. Our becomings
are not identical; you shouldn't have needed
so much courage. But I'd have questions
that I hadn't when you wanted me. I'd tell
you the moment my ankles rejected,
out of principle, the stilettoes you once loved.
How I started listening to each tired muscle's
complaint of a work-pay-off imbalance.
We'd talk about this the way I imagine
adult siblings bond over the likes & differences
of their children. I say "imagine" because
I don't have siblings. Meaning, if you were here
on my porch stoop, our children playing inside,
I'd come out to you first, like I am on the page
right now, as not *her*, still not knowing what
that means. But I'd tell you about the luxury
of carrying less, of collecting more time
to do what neither of us expected. You'd look
at me differently, so differently, say you were
proud without saying it.

rental car

is everything splendid borrowed?
you let me read your Rita Dove books
& i didn't write in them
knowing i would have to return
each cracked spine to your shelf.
your room smelled like cactus candle
& brushed teeth. the window laughed
flecks of car tire alley way.
do you miss what you took from me?
i miss removing your shirts
from the laundry bag before you got home.
i would wear them like dresses
& then place them back, fumbling
to fold them as they came. last autumn
when i was made of different
less vibrating molecules
i rented the car i drove to my parent's house.
grey rain spit water constellations
on the windshield.
the radio came in clear as a knife.
i plugged my phone in & played
Death Cab for Cutie's *Plans* from start
to finish. i pretended
the car was mine even though i only had
four days with it. i forget why
i even came home. the drive from
New York to corn field Pennsylvania

dwindled me to nothing but urges.
i wanted to stand in the backyard. i wanted
to walk the dog all the way over
the waning moon. staring at the car
in the gravel driveway, it looked terribly
out of place. all shiny & white &
fresh. the insides smelled translucent.
the headlights cut holes in my father.
i said i missed you when i didn't.
i was only thinking about missing the car
& missing this American gasoline freedom.
in my parent's house, we wear couches down
until their stomachs touch carpet.
i do the same. let my shoes come to pieces.
sand my heart down to a mirror.
i took my brother on a ride
around the block & i considered
car dealerships. all their newness.
i envied all steering wheels.
you were at home toe-deep in
your own private encyclopedias
& maybe sitting by your window. i missed
your ankles. i missed your closet.
tragic ride home. goodbye beautiful life.
the car key like a talisman. you can
come in & out of love with someone several times
just on the same highway. my life still fits
in back seats of cars i don't own.
turned the radio into a boy &
let his voice lie to me. i gave back
your books one by one without telling you.
in the morning, i dropped the car off
& walked home up Jericho Turnpike
that dreary Monday. car horns squawked
like tired old birds.

distortion

let's run between cars on 5th avenue.
headlights like quarters to spend
on the afternoon heat machine.
once we were racing on the new jersey turnpike
& we should have disintegrated but didn't.
sever the radio into equal fourths.
one for you one for me. car legs
warbling like song birds.
i hung the stop light around my neck
to make you laugh. red comes
like a wide afternoon. you tell me
to read your lips in the honk
of the dead birds. all i can see
you saying is, "maybe maybe."
your teeth are doors i want to pull open.
we play tag in the tremoring city.
no one has eyes anymore. we are using
magnificent implants that only show
objects that smell pleasant.
there aren't enough trains so
only glossy people come & go.
in the rear view mirror our
mothers are singing without sound.
the pigeons are in the trunks
we have to let them out. a simple lock
stands between me & a love poem.
staring into the car-blur i can almost see

an animation of a balloon leaving
a boy's hand. in the morning
all i want is the right spoon.
at night, please give me someone
who worries about yellow as much as me.
the tv stopped asking questions
& now is just an eye piece.
i periscope through lunch & catch
a glimpse of tomorrow
i wasn't supposed to see yet.
i love ruining surprises. do you miss
the sound of the can opening?
a stray dog bites a lamp post down.
none of us are flattened
but all of us are unrecognizable.
mirrors spit us back out & fold
like pocketbooks. there's a wild
twenty dollar bill in the bush or
is that just a kiss of weed?
tell me, what is it you want to see
less clearly? i want to stand
on either side of the street
as cars crackle & spit & try
to say your name
while you try to say mine.

Photo by Ben Katarzynski

W*RK

A first date should always consist of a few things: shaved legs; an attention-grabbing outfit (preferably floral and cake pink); a sunshine attitude, even if it's strained; and one accessory that makes me seem cool but is actually there to cover up a deep insecurity. See: WASP-y non-prescription glasses and my wide-set eyes. Some first dates end in lazy-eyed ugly-bumping at my studio or theirs. I cranked out the first two years of college before getting burnt out forever. I graduated with a degree in Biology, but it hasn't been kind. I don't know what I want to do, but I have to pick a direction and step on the gas. Maybe I should've gone the software engineer route like everyone on Reddit.

Another kind of first date leads to four more dates, meeting friends and family and the IT guy, and then maybe an offer. It's called The Job Hunt. Or, if I'm feeling romantic, The Career Quest, Expedition, Excursion, whatever helps me sleep at night. Sometimes, three dates in, I think it's going well. Joke's on me.

It's been a year since graduation, and I'm still looking for a way to eat. I rent a studio with my hypochondriac roommate who stockpiles his mom's Lisinopril and takes it whenever he feels like he has "emotional fog." He gets by as an admin assistant in a small printing company. I'm jealous when I hear about his waning will to live every time he has to unload reams of paper.

This is my third interview with Jasmine, for a research assistant position at a small biotech company. It'll pay higher than minimum wage. Ten dollars an hour, which is a step up from the grocery store job I'm working. I haven't quit yet, but my boss knows something's up. He hasn't stopped scheduling me for early mornings.

Jasmine and I meet at a bar. It could double for any generic modern restaurant. Wooden counters, geometric log stools, off-menu cocktail drinkers in mustard beanies and wire frame glasses. The TV plays the news, droning on about "the coronavirus" and how to avoid it. The symptoms sound mild. Nobody knows whether to wear masks. I shrug it off.

"You look exquisite, Tess," Jasmine says, purring. Her tongue dips into her cider. "You took advantage of that subscription box, didn't you?"

I thank her. "Oh, *yeah*. Love the essential oils." My skin care routine hasn't changed. It's still just old bar soap. I'm wearing nude heels and a pink dolman sleeve jumpsuit. Same hideous outfit as yesterday. My black hair is dry from hair spray and greasy at the roots. These days, it's winged eyes, stress sweat for that dewy look, and severe, straight brows to blunt my emotions. Editorial, I guess.

The last time I saw Jasmine, we barely discussed the position. We went to 505 Taqueria, which she likes to shit on for being run by bleach-white people from Minnesota in a city steeped in better taquerias. Nevertheless, she demolished a fried avocado monstrosity and listened to me as I confessed how exhausting the interview process was, regretting it immediately. She was sympathetic for a moment. Then, she texted me a list of links to her favorite self-care subscription boxes and services. A list amok with Medium blogs and sexy pastel tone websites. Hundred dollars for meditation. Two hundred dollars for quarterly makeup boxes that don't match shades—no wonder Jasmine's sporting BB cream four shades too light. Forty dollars a month for skin serums that amounted to generic Target oils and moisturizers. At this point, my friends say I'm her unwilling girlfriend. But I hold on, because *maybe* she'll give me a job.

Oh, and then I let her despair-monologue about her meaningless life after she told me I smelled like cinnamon like her ex, Coriander. Gwyneth Paltrow must've consulted on that name. I would've ended the interview but Jasmine's so delectably pitiful, especially over Pall Malls. Jasmine only smokes those nasty cigarettes because Coriander loves them. The woman is thirty-five but smells like tobacco and death. I cry-masturbated on the futon later that night and fantasized about her calling to tell me I'd gotten the job.

Jasmine orders me a cider and goes on about how she started her career in chemical engineering and how she ended up in biotech. "My mom knew the CEO at the company, so he immediately promoted me from intern to engineer," she says. "That's when Cori started to drift. She was always a little bored with me."

"I know we talked about this briefly last time, but I really want to know what you bring to the table. Give me a pitch," Jasmine says. She mutters at the end of her sentences, distracted and half-invested. This time it's the septum-ringed bartender winking at customers. Cider dribbles from Jasmine's chin and onto her trousers.

I say everything the internet experts tell me to say. Talk myself up about marketable skills, lie about my experience, and always, always, always tell the interviewer about how I'm a passionate self-starter, ready to change the world in a lab, slicing rat brains for ten hours in exchange for fifty bucks (after taxes) and some lint.

Her fanged smile tests my reserve for bullshit. "Tell me about a time that you handled conflict."

I've rehearsed this in my car enough times. "Well, when I worked at Gardner's Grocery—"

Jasmine squints. "God, you enunciate your words just like Cori."

I refold the dog-eared corners of my resume. "I know, you said so."

"We've already gone over your grocery store stuff, Tess. It doesn't highlight any skill."

A belch of laughter escapes my mouth. "Work is work, isn't it?"

"Oh, Tess. I didn't mean to offend you, I'm just—"

My patience burns up. "My boss used to cut my hours if I didn't drink with him. How I handled that conflict is I got drinks with him, passive-aggressively ransacked the Kraft mac and cheese, and dealt with it."

To my surprise, her plum-lipped mouth loosens up. "OK, point taken."

I should've stuck to a stale story about communication and empathy and hand kissing and bowing down to the evergreen capitalism gods.

I drone through forty minutes of her nonstop questions, which are all predictable and insurmountable. Who knows what they want in ten years?

She pulls out her phone, effectively ending the interview and negating any questions I have. HR should get back to me next week.

"They told me I'd know by the end of this week."

"I will let you know when I make my decision," Jasmine says, signing the receipt and stuffing her credit card back into her thin wallet.

I go on. "You won't drag me through sixty interviews and ten assignments and then not even have the common courtesy to call and tell me that I didn't get the job?"

"Let's not," she says dryly. "Look, I know the job market is tough out there, but sometimes you just need to wash it down with a couple of drinks and call it a day. My place. What do you say?"

I should say no, but this is just part of the job application labor, isn't it?

Jasmine makes the same face as my other interviewers when I get too enthusiastic. My last interviewer, Nick, a man with a red face that looked like it was pumped full of water, massaged my shoulders after he got a chance to look over the test assignment he'd given me. "Look, you just don't have enough experience. But you should know that Asian women have one of the highest earning potentials in the country." He stopped. "Has anyone ever told you that you look like Sandra Oh?"

Post-grad, my backbone dissolved, and I became a self-disrespecting octopus. Naturally, I invited Nick to a club after the interview, out of shallowly buried insecurity to *please* people.

I threw a sizzling vodka soda on him after he confessed how lonely he'd been feeling, cheating on his fiancée, with his hand on my breast. Smash cut to me chasing Nick down the street to his car, rain stinging my eyes and taking my mascara with it. I lobbed my heels at him and shredded up my resume with my teeth. "I'm a fast learner. I'll take 20%

less than market value!" He sped off in his sexy black BMW and blocked me on LinkedIn. *The kiss of death.*

Jasmine's quaint Taylor Ranch house has all the mid-century modern touches. Bony chairs, boxy couches, long coffee tables, geometric lamps and sculptures, and avant-garde blobs of color paintings reek of her paycheck. The place smells of sweat and is filled with young people who are almost certain to be convicted of embezzlement or assault in the future. She puts on Coriander's "sad daze :-/" Spotify playlist and breaks out the Pall Malls. Phoebe Bridgers sings about being sad. We chain-smoke by the pool.

She coughs like salt on asphalt. "Ah, nostalgia." Jasmine holds me hostage, thumbing through Coriander's Instagram. She's a vampiric redhead with sinewy arms, her knees and elbows capped with pads, standing on a clear penny board. "Guess she forgot to delete this pic." A younger, darker Jasmine beams up at Coriander, sitting on the shoulders of two glitter-smeared ladies. "That night, she was supposed to take me out to celebrate our one year. But we ended up going to this show she wanted to see." I follow Jasmine back into the house and into her bedroom.

The rest of Coriander's feed is filled with reviews of her company's skin care subscription box and her popping, serumed cheeks—a combo that feels like overkill. Striking poses with her posse, all long hair parted down the middle, flashing their teeth, hiding the Pall Malls, searching for the same angles over and over. Numbing the roundhouse anxiety of their emotional labor away, but fashionably.

Jasmine sits me down on her bed. A motorcycle roars through the night air. The space between us vibrates with her only ambition.

I half expect her to deliver a rousing speech about my lack of work experience and how I make up for it in chutzpah and wide-eyed desperation. But people always disappoint. She kisses me. I blurt, "I thought you wanted—"

Jasmine parts my thighs.

"—professionalism."

The sex is utilitarian and thankless. She pounds me from the back, mechanically and breathlessly, and I cover a yawn with my clammy, alcohol-stung hand.

A surprisingly poor performance. She finishes and we drown into slumber.

Three weeks pass and I interview for another lab position and one for research, both hundreds of miles from Albuquerque. The news churns on. China has been shut down since January. It's already here in the States. Someone died from the virus in Washington. It's in New York. Masks should be required in public.

Jasmine strings me along and says I'm a *finalist* for this job. My roommate kept me up until 1:00 a.m., brewing up a storm about the lymph node behind his left ear. The universe does not let up and it does not forgive, so naturally, Jasmine calls me at 5:00 a.m. It's Monday and I'm expected to open up at the store.

"I want to call Coriander."

"OK," I stammer. "Do what you want."

"But I can't call her. Every time I get the urge to call, I stop myself."

In strange situations like this, I don't ask questions anymore. I know my dire circumstances have no room for reason nor rationale. "You've stopped yourself every time, so how's this different?"

"Would you go down to a catacomb speakeasy or a rooftop pool bar?"

I play the game. "Catacomb speakeasy. But alcohol and pools, why not?" I say.

Jasmine sighs like her favorite sunscreen is out of stock. "She would've chosen the catacomb, too. She liked to talk to strangers when she wandered off."

"Without you?"

"I don't blame her. She always had something more important to do, someone more interesting to talk to, someplace better to go. I was just the baseline, and I knew it."

I squirm into a blue A-line skirt, pairing it with a blasphemous emerald green blouse. "Why did you stay?" I wipe my crusty mouth. My gums are dry.

"Isn't it obvious?"

"No."

None of this made sense to me. I would've mourned for my six-month relationship with Santino, this canoe-chinned Argentinian guy in my organic chemistry class, but he was checked out and so was I. I was halfway through my nihilistic phase. Only art house drama films ending in death mattered to me.

"If we'd stayed together, I'd be so different." She coughs into the phone and asks, "You want to make six figures?"

"Depends on where I'm living and what—"

"Yes or no?"

I admit defeat. "Yes." Inevitably we'd meet up and I'd end up tolerating her sweat for forty-five minutes.

Jasmine brags about raking in a 100K salary, but it's not like it matters. Apparently, she's still drunkenly sobbing over Coriander every few months. And buying fugly little worm-shaped vases to crowd her lonely house.

Right after my shift, we meet for lunch at a noodle shop across from the university, because Coriander used to cook luxurious bowls of tonkotsu ramen. Jasmine looks over my resume and gives me unsolicited tips on interviewing. We smoke cinnamon-flavored cigarettes on the patio, the iron table pressing into the undersides of my thighs. I pull my skirt down, flashing the dreadlocked cyclist passing through in the process.

"Look, you just need to act like you want the job more," Jasmine says.

"How much more could I say that I want the job, short of begging and groveling?" I ask.

"If you want to make any sort of living, you have to beg. And speak more like someone who has had a real job," Jasmine instructs.

"You want me to say shit like '*synergy*.'"

Jasmine waves her hand up, eyes glued to her phone. Coriander posted a new picture on Instagram. "That's more like it," Jasmine mutters. "Oh, my God. She's in the city. She's staying at the Silva."

How pathetic. I picture Jasmine checking into the same hotel as Coriander, because fuck her own house, right? She'd be up in her room on the same floor, mixing herself a drink according to a self-care subscription box (complete with a cocktail manual, a smelly berry-snail-juice-wombat-blood face mask, a few rainbow scrunchies, a watery melon-scented lotion, a sugar scrub, a candle that says YOU ARE A BEAUTIFUL SOUL. YOU ARE LOVED AND DESERVE GLITTER AND BLISS, a bag of melted dark chocolate squares, and a bullet journal for daily affirmation) and drafting letters to send to Coriander, just a few rooms down. And then, of course, Coriander spends the night with some other woman, just out of Jasmine's reach. In a depressive, crying lurch, Jasmine would start getting more sophisticated about her self-care. She'd start stacking and staggering her routine: the first month, a subscription box for hipster plantain chips, three months later, for rare cigars, one month after that, for craft bourbon, two weeks later, for steak, and then for butters around the world, ready to lube her arteries so she can finally feel alive. She puffs cigars, sizzles steaks, and spreads butter on entire baguettes, her mouth full of despair and "fuck my therapist!"

All for some idealized version of Coriander that she thinks she's in love with. She's out here pissing away all the money in the world while I kiss ass, trying to convince hiring managers that I want to use my biology degree to do data entry.

Maybe Jasmine does deserve the kraken mouth of this mythical Coriander monster. She has nothing to lose. Reach out and more than likely Coriander won't respond or care. But at least Jasmine can stop being so repulsively frantic and do her damn job. I'm exhausted, depleted of hope, and bitter.

I blurt it out. "I think you should reach out to Coriander." I reach forward and grab Jasmine's hand, rattling my chair against the pavement. "She was too young to know that you were the love of her life. And you were too young to get her back."

She waves me off. "Stop changing the subject." Jasmine continues circling bullet points on my resume. "You need to use better buzzwords. Use 'dedicated.' Or 'optimization.'"

Snatching my resume from her, I seize her phone.

"I'm serious," I say, lifting her phone to show her Coriander's perfectly curated photo feed, acai bowls and beaches porn. "She's here and you're here. Just a few miles apart. If this isn't a sign, nothing is."

"You really think so?" Jasmine's eyes flicker with optimism.

Blech. Not even a hint of doubt. Whatever happened to self-awareness? "Really. Listen, you should call her."

"How? She probably doesn't even have the same number."

"Oh, we can find it. Let me Joe Goldberg this."

"We haven't spoken in, like, ten years! This is crazy." She takes her phone back. "This is crazy, right?"

"You're just too scared to tell her. And now look at yourself, barely functioning, and crying into your bank account." Life goals.

Jasmine slurps down the rest of her noodles. She's ready.

Coriander's number is listed on a random PDF from her company. I drive Jasmine back to her house, where I nearly tackle her when she tries to bring the hard liquor out. She needs to be sober when Coriander rejects her soundly. We sit on the scratchy blue sofa, facing our hazy reflections in her giant TV.

Jasmine punches in her number and calls. Sent to voice mail, twice. I suggest that she send Coriander a long, heartfelt message on Facebook. Then, on Instagram. And every other account that she exists on.

"She's clearly ignoring me," Jasmine sighs. "I mean, hell, I don't even pick up on candidates half the time. And I just screen numbers I don't know."

"When did you hear an outright rejection? She didn't pick up the phone. Think of it like a job," I croon, laughter brimming between my teeth. "Call her again."

This time, the call goes straight to voice mail. It's extremely anticlimactic. I'd hoped to hear Coriander, telling Jasmine to fuck off and to move on with her life. Jasmine could finally stop trolling at bars, blowing snot bubbles and drawing L-word charts to prove to herself that she was happy without Coriander. She's not.

"She blocked me." Jasmine turns her phone over and shuts her eyes.

"Did she? Or did she turn her phone off?" I ask.

She's unsure. "I still love her so much."

I resist the urge to twist my face into disgust. My fingernail drags along the fabric of her couch. "She's at the Silva tonight, isn't she?" I raise my eyebrows. "What's stopping you?"

She pushes back as a formality. "My job. My life. My dignity. A lot. A lot is stopping me."

But it ends when I ask her how much she really wants to be with Coriander. How much she really wants this fever dream to come true. It doesn't take much pushing.

Before Jasmine books it to the Silva, I urge her to get into her glitziest outfit. She needs to put the work in, to reap the benefits. She needs to be sporting the most uncomfortable dress, the most constricting heels, and the frizziest curls to face Coriander. There's *almost* nothing more humiliating than getting ready to get curbed.

Jasmine's closet is atrocious: cobwebs cooped up in every corner, encroaching on the shoe rack (full of gaudy yellow and white and red heels), wrinkled shirts squashed to one side, athleisure wear interspersed. I put something together. Maroon peplum dress, because someone thought that was a good look at some point but that was never true. Black strappy heels.

I drop her off at the Silva and I don't look back. "Good luck," I call out. She'll have to find her own ride back.

It's 7:00 a.m. I didn't sleep much. My email chimes with three automated rejections from jobs I didn't want. The news is eventful. SXSW cancelled a week ago. Dr. Sanjay Gupta is answering questions about COVID-19. Toilet paper is out of stock. The first case has been announced in New Mexico. Jasmine's call cuts through the suspense.

"Tess," Jasmine pants. "Tess, I couldn't do it." The monstrous screech of a shredder bleeds through the phone. "I slept in my office," she admits. "I just could not bring myself to do it. I saw her at the bar and she was sitting alone, and she seemed happy."

"And?" I ask, stirring a cup of tea in the kitchen. My roommate scoots out the door and nods at me.

"I don't know," she says. "When she was right there in front of me, it felt wrong to interrupt. Nothing I said or did could've changed anything. It's all useless."

I pull my lips back over my teeth, like a rodent. I'd been expecting a marvelous crash-and-burn story. This is arguably worse. Self-realization and discovery and *progress*. "How will you ever know if there's a chance for you? You have to go back."

Jasmine sighs. "I can't. I have to move on."

"But won't you wonder?" My tea scalds my tongue and throat.

"I don't think so." Her voice rings. "By the way, I'll see you at 9:00 a.m. on Monday. HR should've sent you some paperwork."

In theory, I should be bounding with joy but it feels like I've limped over broken glass to the finish line. I deserve more, but I'll finally have a full-time job with benefits. I've finally taken the first step. Finally. I smile to myself.

My first week at the company turns into my last week. I've barely made it through the standard procedures training modules and HR forms before Jasmine calls me into her office and lets me go, at the end of the day, of course. I wouldn't be able to do anything for the company working from home.

"Tess, if it's any consolation, you weren't the only one we let go," Jasmine says, spritzing her neck with maracuja oil. A new addition from Coriander's skin care subscription box.

I rush out of the building, the tightness in my shoulders finally relenting. With the ultimate resolve sloshing up to my eyeballs, I stroll into the Taco Bell across the street, my breath in my mask, fogging up my glasses. I order two Chicken Chalupas, one Cheesy Rollup, those seasonal nacho fries which should be year-long, and a big ass Baja Blast. Scrunching the mask off, I unroll the bag of shame in my car, still parked in the company lot. The chalupas are easy to tear through, except for when the tomatoes and sauce drip down my wrist. The acidity stings the web of my skin. The fries and the Cheesy Rollup disappear into my mouth. From the lobby, Jasmine watches me.

It Doesn't Sound Good At All

Now and then, I examine
            my own body. I look for marks,
for evidence that I've been marked.

Honesty is important and something

                        I am quite capable of.
            Just the other day, I was honestly

thinking in a basement
                        every body is buried.
            The earth looms overhead

and all around. I was on my back
                        and beneath my body

a blanket. I stretched my limbs, undoing

            what the day had done
to them. When I was done

                        I dragged the blanket
            up the stairs like a magician
hacking up an endless rag.

Outside—a band of trees
            the neighborhood kids

call a forest. I know something
                        burrowed in the roots
is ready to surface, waiting to

            surround us, to transform
                        its body into a cymbal.

ATS

A month after Hurricane Harvey, rafts of detritus still littered our lives—planks and toaster ovens like ships in bottles bobbing around on people's lawns, lamps in our drives, the gutters brimming with every sort of wretchedness long after the sun was shining again. One of my favorite well-meaning organizations, WMOs, I called them, was setting up on Monday mornings, giving out BBQ at the end of the block. Since I leave my front door open most of the time, Mitch walked right in; my screen door had gone MIA.

He had a clipboard under his arm, the plain old brown kind with a huge metal clip. A ballpoint tied with cotton twine dangled from a hole in the top. In the other hand he balanced two red-and-white checked paper boats of pulled pork, a yellow plastic fork stuck through each. He said, "Knock-knock," but he was already in the living room, already casing my walls, presumably trying to figure out what his slice would be if he got me to sign a contract allowing his company to remove and replace my Sheetrock. I'd seen the guy working the vicinity since the hurricane, easy to spot, always wearing a navy sport coat over a golf shirt.

"Brought you some breakfast, neighbor": that's what he said. The BBQ was already on the big Rubbermaid container I used for storage and for a table, and he was looking around the room trying to find me, or from his perspective, whoever lived there.

When Mitch first walked into my house, I was on two feet envisioning a plumb bob running through the center of my body. I was looking outward, inhaling and exhaling the way I'd learned when I was an undergrad and, needing a single credit, took beginning yoga. In college, half of every class was spent practicing "equal standing." In my living room, I liked to equal stand in the corner, limiting temptation to let my attention wander out the front window. I hadn't practiced it in forty years and as a twenty-year-old had never even achieved enough flexibility to allow me to touch my toes. But to calm myself during Harvey, I'd returned to equal standing like a scrape-kneed toddler to his mother's arms. Sitting in my bathtub, I'd had to modify the idea of standing, pretending my butt cheeks were my feet, grounding myself. But I'd closed my eyes and breathed through the rage for hours. I sat trying to think of nothing, keeping my mind clear, following my breath. "I don't intend to sell you my walls," is what I told Mitch the day he first came. Then I stopped equal standing and stepped out of the shadow, away from my spot in the corner.

I was used to the BBQ WMO feeding us dinner for breakfast; I'd started to enjoy free protein in the morning, so I told Mitch thanks. I wasn't ashamed to take charity but going out of my house required mental energy to face the BBQ volunteers, or any volunteers, the nice people everywhere trying to make things better. They all had scripted questions: *Are you getting along OK?* They tilted their heads in the same understanding way, making me feel like I was being looked after by a bunch of Labradors. *Are things all right today? Have you been to the beach lately?* And, *Hey, do you know what time low tide is this afternoon?* This last question made me paranoid. The volunteers were like EMTs when they ask people who've come to after blacking out if they know who the president is. I never wanted to lie to the well-meaners, nor could I honestly report that I was OK, after the storm, or ATS for short.

"It wouldn't take that much." Mitch pointed his fork at my back wall. He was a fidgety guy, constantly pointing and tapping.

I explained to Mitch—he'd told me his first name by then; I never knew his last—that I had been somewhat prepared. I'm not a Looney Tunes prepper, but a few years before, I'd gotten divorced, and knowing I would have no other place to go in a storm, I bought a generator and fans. When the warnings came before Harvey, I complied with the governor's directive to write my Social Security number on my forearm, since I was committed to staying. Then the big guy arrived and unleashed just the sort of chaos expected of 140 MPH winds, but I didn't die. My house was on the better side of the bay for the particular hurricane hitting shore that day, and my walls stayed standing. They showed deep stains, like ghosts were having a dance on the Sheetrock. But I managed to keep the mold back afterward.

"I rode it out," I told Mitch.

"Same," he said. ATS, it was like we were all walking around with black eyes. Like everyone owed everyone else an explanation for the visible damage from a terrible thing that had happened to them. I didn't tell Mitch about how yoga breathing had carried me through. We were still eating, sitting on two folding camp chairs I had on either end of the Rubbermaid. We could have been mistaken for old pals, which was another ATS vibe, unspoken understanding among people, otherwise strangers, who'd been through variations of a shared hell disaster. Mitch looked at me over his paper boat. I didn't trust him or not trust him either.

"Lot of fraud going round," is what I said. I pointed to Mitch's clipboard and the papers curling up from it. There'd already been thievery around Rockport and all the way up the coast and where the floods had been bad inland to Houston, with contractors accepting down payments then disappearing.

"But you've seen me, right?" Mitch shrugged like a teenager caught stealing a beer from his parent's basement fridge. "I live less than a half mile over." He named the street. "Promise. In a Winnebago with a new square of Astroturf out front. I'm not going anywhere. I'll come back next week, if you want. Let's get you fixed up, all right?" I knew he was talking about getting the house fixed up, but he said get *you* fixed up, like me myself, my body, or my mind.

Mitch reminded me of Desi Arnaz and Ricky Ricardo, an actor playing himself, a guy dressing a part to be the character he already was. Plus he had slicked back hair and a big white smile. But it was also obvious he needed a new razor and maybe he didn't own a car; I couldn't memorize his license plate to report him later if he screwed me over. I felt sorry for him and still glad for the BBQ delivery. "Come back anytime," I said. I held up the plastic bag inside a cardboard box I used for garbage since my trash can blew away, and he threw in his tableware on the way out. "Door's pretty much open," I said.

I hadn't divulged any details about my home insurance and what it was going to pay. I was leery of ceding to anyone whatever ground was still mine. I mused that Mitch had opened communication basically by telling me he wanted to knock my walls down. Watching him stroll away, I determined to keep my blotched but dried Sheetrock standing, and right then the idea came to me to start work on a thing I named my time knot.

That same day I met Mitch, I measured up four feet from the floor and drew a line in Sharpie east to west across the back living room wall and made an arrow point at each end. I started drawing outward from the arrow to my left as I faced the wall. I suppose I was stricken by artistic impulse, a once-in-a-lifetime for me, but the itch hung around as long as I kept the time knot in my thinking, and now, almost two years ATS, it covered half the wall, a spectacular, contorted history of my ordinary life.

I wrote dates on the line, then off of those added drawings, lists and bullet points, occasionally a painstakingly crafted sentence. As its ink ran out, I glued each dead Sharpie to the floor trim. The markers stood along the bottom of the big picture like soldiers or blades of grass. I spent pleasant, distracted eons staring at the blank space considering what additions to make to the time knot. I loved the name I'd given my work, a piece that moved through minutes and years at a pace I alone controlled—that was the time part. A piece that fastened me tightly, helped keep me moored in the ebb and flow of everything ATS—that was the knot part. Sometimes, for the time knot, I needed arrows and thought bubbles and flow charts. I stood on a stool to reach available blank spaces. I worked carefully, not wanting to make a mess of my life. I used Sharpie to ensure things would last.

ATS, thinking I might someday use it to nap on the beach, I'd accepted a portable cot from a WMO. I slept on that in the front room, trying to fill my dreams with inspiration. Since our first meeting, Mitch never missed dropping in on Mondays, so Sunday nights I would lie on the cot rehearsing how I would explain to him what I'd most recently rendered on the time knot.

In a way that was gratifying to me, a month or so after I had begun it, the wall started to resemble a plastic place mat I had that was also a map of Wyoming. I'd filched the place mat many years before from a diner in Cheyenne, and Elaine and I duct taped it to the ceiling of the camper top for my pickup, under which we'd slept on our honeymoon trip across the U.S. On the map, the square state sported objects and city names in a collage of large and small comic strip and Old West styles. Toward the bottom and central, a Mr. Magoo-looking character sat bare chested and bald in a hot spring pool. Yellowstone and Devils Tower marked the upper corners. Cattle roamed everywhere, tumbleweeds, a few oil wells. Dead center, a guy in a cowboy hat rode an outsized, bridled rainbow trout as if it were a bucking horse; I thought of that guy as my mascot. On the bottom I-80 made a thin stripe, like that first line I'd made on my wall, all the way across. Now the map was tacked to the lower left corner of the time knot, referenceable as both an artifact of my marriage and a lesson in cartoon-style drawing.

I'd explained about the map to Mitch after I'd recovered it, unripped, still on the ceiling of the camper, which I had spotted a week ATS crumpled against a palm tree in a beach parking lot. I left the top, grateful for the opportunity to abandon my junk anonymously and steal away with the place mat. That had been many months previous, but maybe Mitch was factoring this story of me looting my own property, or any number of other accounts that might testify against the solidity of my mental state, when he covered for me by delivering a favorable assessment of my condition to a neighbor I barely knew, Judy. I saw everything from my bathroom.

I was taking a leak and craning toward the high-up window looking for birds when I spied the two of them on the back corner sidewalk. Judy's arms flailed around in the direction of my house. I cupped my ear in time to hear Mitch saying, "OK. OK. I promise he's OK." Standing in my john with my fly still down, I put a hand to my chest to verify my OK-ness.

Like a Linus blanket, Mitch held his clipboard. I could only catch a few of Judy's words, making it sound like she was reciting a list. "Graffiti, Ned, light, sometimes! worried, funny, worried, think! tree, writing, concerned, night, never! care, doing?" Judy waved her hands from her waist to the air in front of her like an old comedian.

In a fit of self-assessment, I sniffed my armpits, which I was relieved to find not smelly. I gandered down my front. My shorts looked clean enough. My hands were stained here and there with misplaced, black Sharpie strokes, some new, some older, but I found no evidence of having lost track of myself.

I was still brooding about Judy when Mitch came around the front and in my door that day, pulling his junky aviators off his face sideways the way he always did. I grabbed up a Sharpie and waved it at him. For a few minutes every week, we acted together in this play, sharing backstage camaraderie, the kind of understanding people need in order to present a story together. We'd fallen into this ritual, a grab at normalcy ATS when we met and both of us were undoubtedly lonely and disoriented. Understandable. And it wasn't just Mitch and me. Whole towns had been mangled, neighborhoods in Port Aransas up to their waists in ocean, people wearing other people's clothes. For a long time ATS it was like that, everything visible and invisible also askew, something in everyone dislodged and rearranged. So we each counted on the other guy to deliver his lines and make the right gestures at the right time. That's what I thought was going on.

I shook my head no at Mitch's clipboard to say hello. In return he said, "I'm gonna tell the commission. I am going to do it today, right after I leave." He pointed around the room to the big, billowing stains on my east and west walls and at my linoleum peeled up and desiccated in ridges across the kitchen floor. "You'll have to hire my guys. No way is this place habitable." He said the same thing every Monday like he was reading from a cue card.

On the time knot, I'd worked up to illustrating a time just after Elaine and I decided to go all in for this Texas house. We'd bought the place and were at ease in our new scene. The coastal culture agreed with us—the whooping cranes, the second home. "I am finally getting to the good part," I told Mitch.

My sketch had three trees the way they looked when they'd arrived from the nursery in huge black buckets, ready for planting. We had done a little research about the growth rate of live oaks and the space they might eventually take up, and I'd tried to talk sense into Elaine. But she insisted, like there was no other kind of tree in the world but live oaks. We were a little drunk on the idea of longevity, the idea that these trees would be providing protection and oxygen long after we died, something close to forever. Elaine and I held hands when they arrived, backing up together while the truck backed into our driveway.

Mitch presented me with a brand-new Sharpie, which he said he had filched from his boss's desk drawer. "Special for you," he said. He was making me think that Ricky Ricardo thing: perfect smile, gorgeous hair, expressions on demand. I wished I could put a carnation in the lapel of his blazer or tie a bow tie on him to affirm how right I was. I also wondered if he'd swiped the pen from Walgreens.

"I'm working on my ex-wife's trees." I stepped aside and did the Vanna White to show him. It was a small drawing, and he leaned in to have a look at the date: October 2012.

"Seven years ago," he calculated.

I told Mitch that they were Elaine's trees. But they were our trees, really, both of ours. I didn't specifically want something other than live oaks, and I had acquiesced because she'd been adamant. Then I gave in and let her spend about six months' savings on the three trees when I thought one big plant had a better chance at surviving forever, like we'd been envisioning. One would be a more consolidated investment is what I told Elaine, like putting money in a single account to earn the most interest. "That's how we got here!" I pointed out. I was a civics teacher, not a finance guy, but I'd invested. We weren't close to wealthy but retired three years early with a livable pension and with this new place by the Texas sea! Elaine said I sounded like a realtor. I said a larger root system would also be more supportive to a heavy trunk in the long run.

But Elaine had taught little kids, and she countered with not putting all our eggs in a single basket, and we went with what she wanted because she cared about it more. She named this kind of ruling a "group decision."

Group decision, GD I called it, was the ironically dubbed conjugal code for a thing that was non-negotiable and therefore an issue we didn't need to waste time or energy quibbling over. Initially it referenced Elaine's GD to be childless, a choice I thought was hers to make. She'd been clear about it practically from the moment I met her, that long ago, and had her tubes tied as a wedding present to me so we wouldn't have to fuss with birth control. Anyway, when I agreed to her GD about the live oaks, I knew that she would squeal and clap like a kid, a mannerism of hers that made my heart flutter and which she sometimes still did at 62, and which she performed unprompted at the nursery after we'd hand-picked the trees we wanted.

"What happens when you finish?" Mitch pointed to the line where my graying Sheetrock met the trim, where the sun would go down if my time knot was a day. By then I thought he understood that I knew he had no job or boss. He'd started wearing a cheesy name tag from a rental car company pinned to his blazer. It was chipped so that the *h* looked like an *n*, so his name, I thought, would be pronounced like a child saying "mitten." Every week the papers on his clipboard curled up farther.

When I didn't answer, Mitch came close to read the list I was working on. He clapped my back—I think the only time we actually touched. Then he spread himself like an albatross, the end of one finger on the live oaks, the rest of his wingspan measuring the blank space still left on my wall. "Really. What happens when you finish?" His body was extra twitchy. Maybe he felt responsible for me now that he'd promised Neighbor Judy I was OK.

"When I arrive back in the present? At the end of the line, so to speak?" I was adding a flock of flying birds above a representation of my house, flattened letter *M*s across the sky. Mitch looked away, tapping his pen so fast it sounded like a woodpecker, and I knew I'd poked some bruise on him. But we'd ventured way off-script, so I said the truth which was when the time knot was finished, I planned on calling Elaine and telling her straight the fate of the live oaks.

While I'd been yoga breathing in the bathroom during Harvey, I couldn't block out hearing a crash I knew was my big west window shattering. A day later when I stepped out of the tub and opened the door, I was greeted by a plaid easy chair that had blown in and landed upright, like it'd been delivered. I was sitting in that sopping chair falling asleep, pretending to be Archie Bunker. My heart had been still upside down, my ears still full of the roar of tornadoes when Elaine called ATS.

I thought her voice brightened with relief once I'd said I was OK. I was using a stick I found on the floor as a cigar, thinking about if I was Archie, I wouldn't be such a bigot, but then what would be the point of being Archie at all? Plus there was no chair in my front room for Edith. Then Elaine told me, as casually as if she had been saying that we were having broccoli with dinner, that she was selling the house, the place we'd built together thirty years before in Albuquerque. Until she said that, I'd thought in some crooked back alley of my brain that divorcing was just another thing we were doing together. I authenticated this illusion using evidence that we were nice to each other. Neither of us wanted the other person to go on hurting; Elaine made a GD about that. I shouldn't try to make breaking up mean anything other than what it was. No analogies, no abbreviations, she told me. She got Albuquerque, I got Rockport. No sadness. We were so polite. So agreeable. GD.

But we'd never agreed about her abandoning everything and moving to Costa Rica. I was sitting there right ATS in my new Archie Bunker chair with a soaking wet ass and broken glass all over the floor, and I still didn't want her to know that she was making me cry, because that would have made her sad. So I told her that the live oaks had all survived. After the call I went in the yard and took pictures of the holes. There were massive pits where two of them got sucked right out of their places.

I was going to show Mitch the photos on my phone. He was looking at where I'd drawn the trees. But then he pulled in his stomach and tried to stand up tall, the way men do when they're trying to be bigger than you, a thing which wasn't going to work for Mitch, who couldn't have been five seven tops. Plus his shoes were old, and he wasn't wearing socks. "How about when you're done, we sign?" was what he said. Clipboard in hand, he took a few steps back and tapped on the wall trim.

To my discredit, right then I was weighing Mitch's importance to me, how easy or hard it would be to get by in life without him. Maybe he was ready, then, to end our weekly meetings, in a manner of speaking, find a way to finish things between us. For my part, I didn't want to acknowledge how much I relied on him, but Mitch had become a constant in my head. A person, or the idea of a person, who was understanding and acted in the spirit of a friend. A person to whom I could explain my time knot, something like how people talk to God, even when there's no evidence of his benevolence. Unable to summon another response, I shrugged, and said, laughing, for the hundredth time, that I wasn't signing his papers.

Instead, I told Mitch the story of Elaine and the three live oaks. I'd titled it like that in my head before I drew the buckets and the trees on the time knot. A fairy tale, *Elaine and the Three Live Oaks*. Above the trees I wrote, "Larry, Moe, and Curly," making a show of it as Mitch, ever agitated, sat in one of my camp chairs.

As soon as I wrote the names, I put a single neat line through each. "It's what I wanted to call the trees when we first got them." I put the lid on the Sharpie and pointed, using my teacher skills, giving a lesson.

"You named the trees?" Mitch gave a look that made me feel stupid.

"I was joking around," I said in defense.

A couple of delivery guys off-loaded the trees by the holes they'd dug the day before. Elaine didn't like my suggestions, but after I'd said Larry, Moe and Curly, she really went with the name thing. Once they were in the ground, Elaine went from tree to tree, petting the trunks like kittens. I remember it, her in the yard in her baggy Bermudas and this massive sun hat so she looked like something out of a plant catalog.

"How about Faith, Hope and Love?" Elaine skipped. I mean literally she skipped, across the yard, like a little child, over to the biggest tree. "But the greatest of these is Love," she said.

"Jesus." I rolled my eyes. We weren't Christians before, during, or after our marriage. I know that for certain. Although I also thought we were happy, especially here near the shore. I had a middle-aged paunch and ugly toenails; she refused to dye her hair and hated what she called her turkey neck. We both snored if we were sleeping on our backs. Usual stuff. I thought that we were aging together nicely. We spent two winters in the house, identifying birds, walking the beach, watching PBS mystery shows, drinking wine on the porch. We were laughing more, even if we were making love less. It wasn't like we were ever going to be young again. Then we got the trees.

That day Elaine stood in the yard beaming at the live oaks, I said to her, "'Maybe we should call them Father, Son, and Holy Ghost if we're getting religious about it.'"

On the wall above Larry, Moe, and Curly I wrote those names and crossed them out as well because Elaine nixed them while she was hugging that biggest tree. "Too masculine," she said.

"Mind, Body, and Spirit?"

While Mitch watched, I wrote sets of three names on the time knot, each above the previous set, then crossed the names out because Elaine had rejected them.

The trees did look nice, two in front, one in the backyard. That one in the back, the delivery guys warned us, would have to get moved or be cut down in ten years if it grew as expected. Elaine must have known already that she wouldn't be living with me a decade into the future. "Bacon, Lettuce, and Tomato?" I asked her. I was standing on our little strip of sidewalk, out there in my flip-flops like always.

"No." Elaine, barefoot in the grass, gazed up into the branches of Love. She looked ecstatic, I guess. Her names sounded trite to me, even a little daft. But she looked so cute, and I was filled with emotion for her with her familiar, knobby knees showing. Concurrently, my heart had a twitch of sarcastic rage at the thought of assigning names to saplings, even though it had been my idea. All the same, as fast as I could I started popping off trios when I should have let the issue drop.

"Of the People, By the People, For the People?" Elaine shook her head. She had pulled her lips inside her mouth and then smiled, a coy look. "Nina, Pinta, Santa Maria?"

"Faith can be the one in back," she said. "Hope is there." She pointed to the opposite corner of the property where Hope was already sending down its roots. "And this is Love." Elaine kissed the tree.

We were both being ridiculous, but it was fun. And she had the greatest legs, I swear, even then. "All right," I said, "Crosby, Stills, and Nash." Elaine loved Crosby, Stills, and Nash. We must have flipped that tape a thousand times when we were newlyweds driving across the country being idealistic and screwing every night under the Wyoming place mat. Even afterwards when we'd settled down, she loved CSN.

"'Faith, Hope, and Love.' She kept shaking her head at me. Wouldn't even consider my best offer." I turned around then to see if Mitch was grasping all that I was saying. I was fishing for sympathy on account of my ex-wife losing her love for me and putting it toward other things, like trees. But Mitch was looking confused, had his face wixed up about twelve different ways.

"OK. You have to understand now." I walked over to look squarely down on Mitch where he sat in one of my camp chairs. "I'm not going loco if that's what you and my neighbor are acting so bent about." I tried to look calm, tried to relax and push my shoulders back and down, down, down.

So what if I liked writing on my walls? So what? I'd started to come into my post-retirement, post-divorce, 60-something, ATS own. I wasn't hurting anyone. My body buzzed and brimmed with clarity when I worked. It was like solving an enormous, 3-D word puzzle, working across, then down, then jiggy-jack, knowing if I answered a few more clues, I'd unlock the whole problem and get it right. Everything would fit together. I acknowledged to Mitch that I had stumbled on an unconventional strategy for working through my shit, but I wasn't drinking or smoking too much. I had my pension income. I was eating on a regular basis.

Mitch sat there acting like his chest was a drum set. He had a pattern beat: first near his heart, then on the shirt pocket where his aviators lived, which made a little jangle. "Oh, they're worried, all right." Mitch did the heart-aviator rhythm sequence between sentences. "It's not just Judge Judy out there, either. She says the whole hood is talking about you. Now it's on me to make sure you don't crack."

"Crack?" I envisioned how little chicks crack out of eggs to get a start. I walked over and stood in front of the time knot and stretched my arms out like Christ the Redeemer way off in Rio. I was feeling large, but suddenly small and sad, and I let my arms fall down. "Because of this?" I loved my wall. "I'm putting my life back together," I said. Mitch was still drumming on himself.

He stared past me at the time knot a while. It looked amazing with its twists of words and dates and pictures, the kinks and snarls of my experience. Finally, he said, "I'm not worried," and he put his head on the Rubbermaid like when an elementary school teacher tells someone to put their head down on the desk. "Not worried at all," he said. Then he dropped his clipboard on the floor and was blubbering, and I felt bad for never asking if he was OK, probably ever.

Still, I didn't want to say anything about him crying or ask him what was wrong because what the hell kind of a question would that have been? I avoided looking at Mitch and spent the next few minutes staring at the time knot considering where I'd make the next lines. Up to then, I'd used about half the wall to show most of my life, but I hadn't come yet to the hurricane. I was in my head working over this issue of space relative to time when Mitch stopped crying and asked me if I knew where the wheelchair was.

The wheelchair was busted, sitting on the side of a debris pile left on what had been a vacant lot, in a medium-priced neighborhood, like mine, a half mile from the shore. It was a landmark, a touchstone, ATS, a thing to look away from and look back at after passing.

The wheelchair had been facing uphill for the nearly two years ATS, the hill being a junk mound, like others around town comprised of two-by-fours and metal shorn from appliances, branches with long-dead leaves still clinging, moldy furniture, DANGER and KEEP OUT signs written in spray paint on delaminating plywood. How it rested, the smaller front wheels for steering lost in garbage. The two big back wheels bent crazily, looking like tiny Tilt-a-Whirls. "Yeah. I know where the wheelchair is," I said.

Uneasy about seeing Mitch undone, I kept my eyes on the wall. It was the first time I'd given a thought to the guy having some kind of time knot of his own unraveling from inside him.

A few days before, Mitch had seen the wheelchair lifted away. He described the crane arriving, the workmen circling the debris pile, guiding the guy in the cab. This process was usual by then, SOP. The newspapers and the WMOs said that people would feel better once the ruins were hauled away. They judged that we longed to have our city out from under the weight of our former existence. The social workers told us it would be better, psychologically, to have our memories, since they were so battered, removed. In the streets people looked on at the machinery hoisting up chunks of their lives. We were supposed to believe things would go back to the way they were before if we could account for what we'd lost and what we'd managed to hold on to. Mitch said he'd stood on the opposite corner, just outside where workers had put up the caution tape.

"The chair just hung there," he said. "Then there was some kind of problem, and the guys running the operation left the claw in the air, holding on to the wheelchair." Mitch wiped his face on the sleeve of his blazer. "For ten or fifteen minutes it was like that, and a few people walked by and took pictures because it looked like someone, a person I mean, got dumped out. Like a carnival ride gone bad, and then I couldn't move my feet, you know? You know?" he kept asking me. I thought I knew what he meant. Someday we might be in wheelchairs, or our wheelchairs would be broken, or we'd have to rely on others, no chance to decide for ourselves how to stick out a storm? Maybe that's what he was thinking about.

"You know?" he said. "Then they got back to work, and the chair just went in the dumpster like nothing. And I felt like I had to stay there until the whole pile was picked up, and pretty soon it was past lunchtime and all the rats that had been living underneath the garbage had run away down the street, and the work guys waved when they left me."

A flop of his Desi hair hung all wrong across Mitch's forehead. Averting my eyes to the floor, I saw his clipboard and the papers on it, which were clearly a sheaf of one Lara Stover's junk mail, an advertisement and form for ordering new bank checks with polka dots or flowers, or with faint pictures of wolves, anything a person could want.

That was when I finally told Mitch right out that my place was well-insured. I'd lost plenty of siding and part of the roof and a few big windows. Now it felt like confessing to say that I had made a damage claim on my house right ATS. I did get new windows, but deposited the rest of the money in savings, thinking I'd leave the tarp on the roof and do the walls and floor at a pace that I could pay from my pension income while I kept a growing nest egg in the bank for the next disaster. The visual evidence surrounding us added up to what I was saying. It was time to acknowledge out loud that any insurance I had was not paying him or anyone he knew to tear down my drywall.

After that Mitch sat and rubbed his chin; maybe he was tired of drumming all over himself. His face looked like he was trying to work through a tough math problem without writing anything down. After a while he stood up and went and pointed at the three trees on the wall. "Are you really going to call her?" he asked me, and I told him I believed in my heart that I was.

Mitch took hold of the phony pockets of his blazer and flapped them like he was a polyester bird. The coat had gone shiny with wear in patches. "Who survived?" he asked. He started doing an eeny-meeny-miny-moe thing among the trees, still in their buckets in my picture.

I tipped my head toward the back of my house. If there had not been walls, we could have seen the tree, which had grown a couple of feet since Elaine had gone, and filled in, branched out. "That's Crosby in the back," I said. "Or Faith."

Mitch mimed snorting a long line of cocaine. "Well it's not like that guy's going to last forever," he said. Then he made a gesture to show the approximate dimension of David Crosby's belly.

That night I cut down the time knot without finishing. I found a Swiss Army knife, SAK, that had been in the kitchen drawer since Elaine gave it to me, a gift for our twenty-eighth anniversary, the last before she made the GD to leave me. It had a saw blade, something I had laughed about when I opened the present, disbelieving I would ever need such a thing. I kicked a hole into the wall near the beginning of the time knot. After that I used the tiny SAK saw to work at the Sheetrock, making cuts and pulling out pieces of the puzzle as I could. It took me all night. I cut around my drawing of the trees. The chunk was dusty and jagged and fell apart.

As the pieces came loose, I hauled them on the porch and tossed them into the corner of the yard, the pit where Love had been, or Nash. "You all right, Ned?" It was Judy, walking by as if she walked by every night at 1:00 a.m. Half the time knot was in the yard by then.

"Oh, Judy," I said. I toodled my fingers at her and smiled. I stood up straight. "Hi there, Judy," I said to be sure she heard me before I went back in. I was covered in white dust, the little saw blade in my hand. My knuckles were bleeding.

Before I cut it down, I'd skipped ahead and drawn the end of the time knot. I drew myself as a stick man, no flesh, no body in which to keep guts or a heart. Stick-man me was equal standing and had a conversation bubble, and I cut the whole thing out, wanting to save it for Mitch, sawing in three-inch strokes to preserve what he already knew. The me-guy was saying, "Then Harvey flew over and I hid from death in a fiberglass bathtub." I set that bit on my Rubbermaid and the next day went looking for Mitch where he lived. There was no place like he described, no little trailer with Astroturf on the street where he'd said. I gridded for miles, looking.

Photo by Ben Katarzynski

Benjamin Franklin's Return

Coming down the airliner's airstairs
    he caught sight of our jeans our T-shirts
    and gasped
The jet had brought him from somewhere
    his handlers weren't saying where
the past I suppose
    wherever they keep it these days

As a hundred smartphones flashed their lights
    a blue-shirted officer demanded his passport
Remove your shoes your belt those glasses that hat
    Trying to keep from frowning
he shoved both hands deep into pockets
    until a torn candy wrapper blew against his leg
and one hand insisted
    on picking the strange thing up

Later we answered his questions
    about our masks and why we stood so far away
He attended us with curiosity
    but stared blankly at the words virus and social distancing
When he asked who was president
    we shuffled feet cleared throats changed the subject
His hands unable to make up their minds
    sprang open as if to receive
then snapped closed into two fighting fists

Naturally he requested a diplomat's tour
    of all fine things he'd known in his time
a printing press
    the post office
an insurance company
    betting against a flame's appetite
We had to say all were closed
    closed by the virus
the pandemic the plague

For a long time he stared into those famous hands
    stretched like open books before his paunch
then asked
    But what about kites
Surely on a windy day
    people must still fly kites
Please tell me
    please tell me that they do

Going to Hades

"I told you to bring something homemade. This was obviously bought in a bakery," my mother told her sister, Janice. They were in the kitchen, and Aunt Janice had just handed her a flawlessly latticed blueberry pie on a red plastic plate.

"How do you know?" Aunt Janice asked.

"It's obvious. You couldn't bake something like this."

"Get a grip. It's a *pie*, for God's sake."

"I specifically asked everyone to bring something homemade," my mother repeated. She had potluck dinners with sympathetic friends every Monday night so we could live off the leftovers for the rest of the week.

"Look, if it was that important, I would have baked the pie myself, but not all of us can drink all day like it's a full-time job!"

"Janice, would you like to know what you can do with your pie?" my mother asked.

Since my father had left us after getting another woman pregnant, my mother had been hitting the bottle with an air of entitlement. She mainly drank vodka because it didn't leave an odor, and she was still intent on keeping up appearances which, in our case, was like offering someone a chair in a house that had burned down.

I slunk out of the kitchen into the backyard, but I still heard Aunt Janice yelling since all the windows were open, accusing my mother of living like she was "on Tobacco Road!"

Outside, my sister, Evelyn, was rambling around in our father's toolshed. Our father had been gone for two months and neither of us really missed him or if we did it was in the sense that you mourn a rotten tooth that was pulled. We felt his absence, were relieved he was gone since it was so much quieter. He was a man given to rages like epileptic fits. Today, he probably would have been diagnosed with PTSD, having done a tour of duty in Korea, though I suspect he was wound very tightly to begin with.

I went inside the toolshed and saw Evelyn hovering over what looked like a body. Coming closer, I saw it was a mannequin's male torso with no arms and legs. Its comely head was still intact, and the painted blue eyes blandly stared up at me.

"Where did you find that?" I asked her. In terms of random objects, this was quite a treasure with a lot more potential than tennis balls or even costume jewelry.

"In back of Levy Brothers," Evelyn said. Levy Brothers was a local department store.

"What are you going to do with it?"

"I'm figuring that out," Evelyn said. Evelyn was twelve, only two years older than me, but she seemed like a wizened adult. She was tall and thin, wore charmless bifocals, and in certain lights, her lank blonde hair looked grey. "I'm going to make him Hades, King of the Underworld, and charge kids money to see him."

The week before, our next-door neighbor had told us our family had "gone to Hades," not realizing Evelyn loved Greek mythology. She was specifically referring to our lawn which hadn't been mown all summer. This same woman also called our household "that whole kit and caboodle" which sounded like a bouncy ride in an amusement park.

"What makes you think anyone'll pay to see him?" I asked.

"You know how scared everyone is of going to Hell, but they still go to horror movies, don't they?"

Evelyn was an unabashed fan of *Famous Monsters of Filmland* which she read as avidly as Greek myths.

"It's a dummy," I reminded her. "It's not real."

"So are the statues at Holy Angels Church and people treat them like they're real. Remember Baby Jesus?"

The Christmas before, vandals had kidnapped a Tiny Tears doll from a crèche outside the Methodist church, and people had been as anguished as if it were a live infant. There was even a reward for its return.

"He doesn't look like a monster," I said. He looked like a giant Ken doll.

"I'm going to make him a mask and a crown and then he will."

"What about his arms and legs?"

"Not having them makes him scarier."

She was right. You imagined he had all the fury of someone who'd been dismembered.

"Are you going to keep him in here?"

"I got a better place."

The shadowy clutter of the toolshed seemed the perfect place for the King of the Underworld. In the dark, my father's wrenches and clippers looked like instruments of torture which he'd sometimes threatened us with if we misbehaved.

We left the toolshed and walked over to a gaping pit in our mangy backyard. One night when he was drunk, my father and his friends had dug it. He'd planned to build a swimming pool, but lost interest the morning after. He had a very short attention span, which accounted for his patchy work history, and he'd only stayed with Mom for as long as he had because he was cheating on her constantly. I should mention he looked like Paul Newman, or you wouldn't understand why she'd married him in the first place.

"I'm going to stick a ladder down there, and they can climb down to Hades. Maybe I'll use Beezer as Cerberus." Beezer was our aging, overweight beagle, my father's hunting dog.

"Who's Cerberus?"

"Hades' watchdog."

"How much are you going to charge?"

"It'll depend on how long they stay down there. The longer they stay, the more it costs."

I'd started warming up to the idea of kids daring themselves to descend into a pit to meet a monster. It was definitely better than a puppet show.

"We won't tell Mom or Aunt Janice," Evelyn said.

Our mother would want the money for herself. We didn't get an allowance, and both of us had been banned from the local drugstore for shoplifting candy and gum.

Evelyn got Hades a crown from Burger King when Aunt Janice took us to lunch there that Wednesday.

Aunt Janice was an executive secretary in a law firm, and she'd picked us up straight from work. I thought she was the epitome of chic in her high heels and navy-blue sheath although my mother disparaged her as "an old maid." She was about twenty-six and "getting on" as Mom put it. Later, we found out she'd been having an affair with her married boss for years. He was probably the one who bought her fancy outfits.

As usual, Aunt Janice pressed us for information on the sorry state of our homelife, but Evelyn and I were very loyal to our mother.

At that time, a household comprised of only females was considered a dire situation since the members were completely vulnerable, but all-male domiciles were glorified in *Bonanza* or *My Three Sons* where the atmosphere was robust and freewheeling without a querulous woman to put a damper on life. It strikes me now that Evelyn might have made Hades the man of the house since Daddy had deserted us.

"How are things at home?" Aunt Janice whispered solicitously. We were also on what our grandmother called "relief" and under strict orders not to tell anyone.

"Everything's fine," Evelyn said, savoring her vanilla milkshake as if she'd bathe in it if she could.

"You both seem awfully hungry."

My mother had stopped cooking, and we were living mainly on cereal and mayonnaise sandwiches.

"It's just that we love Whoppers," Evelyn said, and I even started singing a parody of the Burger King song, *"Burger King, Burger King, Burger King—There's a Burger King, right next door, eat a Whopper off the floor—"*

"I'm worried about you two. So is Grandma," Aunt Janice said, tearing up behind her cat-eye glasses. "Grandma wants you to come live with us, but your mother won't let you."

"She needs us," I said.

"Does she, Cheryl?"

"Why can't Mom move in with Grandma?" Evelyn asked. My grandmother's five-room Victorian was certainly big enough.

"Grandma won't tolerate a drinker. Especially a woman, even if it is her daughter. Grandma's father drank."

"Could we get Burger King crowns?" Evelyn asked, changing the subject.

"Sure," Aunt Janice said. "Go ask the girl at the counter."

While Evelyn went to get the crowns, my aunt pressed me for more information.

"What are you girls going to do when school starts again? What are you going to wear, and what'll you eat for lunch?"

"Peanut butter."

She closed her eyes, shook her head, and her red lipstick had smeared so that her mouth looked bloody. Just the sight of us wounded her. We were as pale and messy as children of the Great Depression, not to mention that we probably smelled since we kept wearing the same unwashed clothes. We *were* children of the Great Depression: our mother's.

Once she had the crown, Evelyn made Hades' mask out of papier-mâché. She wanted Hades grotesque but melancholy in the manner of the Hunchback of Notre Dame. In spite of ruling over all those dead souls, he was lonely as if the subjects he really wanted were alive.

"What do you think?" Evelyn asked me when the mask was finished.

Evelyn was a fastidious artist, and she'd painted the mask a somber blue with drooping eyes and thin, rigid lips that seemed to hold every secret in the world. My sister had a real feel for tragedy.

"I like it," I told her.

He evoked an eerie compassion. If life was hard, you looked at him and knew that death was harder, which was why people feared it so much.

In the attic, we found a gold rayon curtain for his cape then climbed down into the swimming pool pit on a ladder and sat him on a cushion there.

The first person to visit him was a boy in my class named Tommy. He was our test subject, and I chose him because he was quiet with an air of discretion that was rare in kids my age. He also lived in a nearly all-male household except for his mother, and I think that made me look up to him. They even had a collie like Lassie though his grandfather had hung himself the year before, which might have accounted for Tommy's general reticence.

Tommy admired the work that had gone into Hades, but said it wasn't like he did anything. He wasn't a ride.

"This is more for little kids," he suggested, perhaps not to hurt Evelyn's feelings. "It might help if you put your dog down there, too."

The next day he brought his four-year-old brother, Richie, to meet Hades, and that little boy brought another kid named Jimmy, and it was Jimmy who became Hades' most frequent visitor.

Jimmy was one of seven children in a jangling household where ordinary conversation wasn't possible. You had to scream to be heard. Aside from the endless clamor, his mother regularly told her children to go to Hell, and this was Jimmy's chance to see the place that she referred to.

On Tommy's suggestion, Evelyn made a gold cape for Beezer and put him in the pit next to Hades.

"This is Hades' dog," she explained to the little kids who visited. "He guards his kingdom. You're only allowed in the front part. The rest is too scary. It would give you nightmares."

Once Jimmy was there, he usually stayed for hours, managing to pay her in nickels and even quarters. We could hear him softly talking to Hades as if confiding secrets or trying to comfort him. We even heard him singing. Other times, he napped next to Beezer.

Jimmy liked it so much he brought other tykes with him as if it just calmed them to be nestled in the earth like baby rabbits no one could reach. We couldn't really figure out what exactly attracted them, and when Evelyn asked, they were too small to explain. They only told her, "I like it here." Maybe it was the idea of meeting a monster in safety. Maybe it was Beezer, or maybe just the peace and quiet mesmerized them.

We didn't really care what their reasons were. Their coins made life more palatable, and it was a lot easier than collecting bottles. We could now afford movies, barrettes, and other niceties our classmates took for granted.

Jimmy's visits seemed to go on for weeks until the day his mother showed up. She was a hefty woman with a black pixie haircut that juxtaposed the difference between her massive body and tiny head. She dragged Jimmy by his forearm while he whimpered.

"What's going on here, Evelyn?" she said severely, sounding as cross as she looked.

"What do you mean?"

"Jimmy told me he comes here to see a troll, and you charge him money to do it. You ever wonder where he gets the money?" Spittle flew out of her mouth like a steam iron. "He's been stealing it from his brothers and sisters and also from me!"

My sister stared at the woman in quiet defiance. Until she noticed loose change was missing, she hadn't even cared where he was. It strikes me now that we were running an early version of a day-care center since preschool didn't exist at that time, a place where the children always felt welcome even if they paid us in pennies. Evelyn was really kind of a visionary.

"I'm not going to bother waking your mother up out of her stupor! I'm telling your Aunt Janice! I want that money back! I estimate that all in all you owe me two dollars!"

As soon as she left, Evelyn climbed down into Hades' lair on the ladder and carried the mannequin up.

"What are you going to do with him?" I asked.

"Hide him in the woods," she said. She spoke as if he was a fugitive that we were helping; I think he had become that real to her.

There was a small stretch of forest near our house where we'd played when we were little. We had to cross the street and walk through a neighbor's yard to get there and luckily the gate was open. Evelyn threw Hades over the broken log fence, then we followed.

We immediately felt sucked into the messy forest as if the houses skirting it didn't exist. The woods were like a whole other world, so cluttered with blighted weeds and grass that the sunlight was hazy. Mushrooms infested the dying trees like tumors and moss grew in green spongy mounds. When I think of it now, it was exactly where Hades belonged.

We walked for a while and found a patch of wild periwinkle flowers, and Evelyn placed the mannequin there, covering him with dead leaves and branches, then we headed back.

When we got home, it was almost evening, and our mother and Aunt Janice were in our little box of a living room. Clearly, there'd been a confrontation. A suitcase stood on the linoleum floor.

As soon as Aunt Janice saw us, she started crying.

"Where have you girls been?" she demanded. "I was going to call the police!"

"Nowhere," Evelyn said.

Aunt Janice handed her the suitcase. "Honey, go pack some clothes for you and Cheryl. You're coming to stay with me and Grandma."

"*No!*" I screamed and ran over to my mother who was standing near our ruined fireplace. I hugged her as if she might float away, but she hardly responded.

"Barbara Moore came to see us," Aunt Janice told Evelyn, cupping my sister's face in her hands.

"Who's Barbara Moore?" Evelyn asked.

"Jimmy's mother. She told me he was paying you money to go down in that pit in the backyard." The way Aunt Janice phrased it made it almost sound evil. "I really don't know what was going on and I'm not going to ask. I gave Barbara the two dollars she said you owed her."

"She's a liar!" Evelyn was outraged. "I don't owe her anything. We were babysitting!"

"It's all right, Evelyn," Aunt Janice said. "She's an awful woman, but you and your sister are still little girls. You need supervision and you're not getting any here. That hole in the backyard should have been filled up years ago. It's a miracle no one fell in and broke their neck. Every time you get in the car with your mother, I'm worried to death."

We were both silent. My mother had hit a parked car once in town, but no one had seen, and we'd driven away.

"The refrigerator is empty except for Wonder bread and mayonnaise," Aunt Janice said.

"I was going to go shopping just before you came," my mother said.

"You're coming to stay with me and Grandma. Even your mother knows it's for the best."

"You don't want to take care of us?" I looked up at her, but my mother didn't answer. She gave me a remote stare as if I were a stray cat trying to ingratiate itself.

"Don't you love us?" Evelyn asked her.

"Of course, I love you," she said.

"Then why can't you take care of us?"

"It's not the same thing," my mother said dully.

Tears rolled down Evelyn's cheeks and Aunt Janice handed her the suitcase.

"Pack whatever you need and we'll buy what you don't have."

Within a couple of weeks, we settled into a new regime of clean clothes, regular meals and daily baths. Aunt Janice worked for lawyers and they filed papers to sue our father for child support. The shock of being completely alone even roused our mother out of her torpor. She started going to AA meetings and, after we moved in, Aunt Janice broke up with her married boyfriend and got engaged to a cop. Maybe she wanted to set a good example for us.

Things improved so drastically it was uncanny. Years later, my sister told me she could only credit Hades for the change as if she'd unwittingly built him a shrine and her desperation had breathed life into him like a golem. Although we never visited our father, we did go back to the woods the next summer to check on Hades, but he wasn't where we'd left him.

There was a small stone house that bordered the forest where two older women lived, and the cottage was somewhat of a landmark since the owners were seen as rarely as coyotes. The rumor was that they were witches, but they were probably just lesbians.

Evelyn and I saw Hades on their front lawn. They were using him as a scarecrow, but he looked more like a sentinel, guarding their place.

Nocturne

Meet me in the dusk
Between the shoulder blades of sailboats
Where I'll let my hair grow long

Along the coral that absorbs
The tattooed rings
Of Saturn's fever

There in the purity
Of liquid obsidian
I'll feed the pyres

Oil and incense
Tarping phosphorus
In soil and incandescence

Meet me in the snow filled cemeteries
Between the liquor of irises
Perfumed in your sweet potato breath

Where the lunar banquets defrost
The frozen appetites
Of the copper pan moons

Where the marble buttons are undone
In your tambourine eyes
Shaking loose the thistles from teeth

There in the passing of the arching fields
Find me in the glass blown poppies
Sacrificed to the gasoline filled volcanos

Where I will dissolve
In your gunpowder mouth
Curating the subterranean art galleries

That snowfall in the nightly songs
Of loneliness and morning moans
Escaping as violins and violet

Draining emerald and lilac
From the raven's throat
I will meet you in the dawn

Where the trees and streams
Crawl along the eternal shorelines
Of renaissance and cities silhouetted

Where the tattooed sun descends
From the nocturnal window
With no one to receive it in their mouth

Photo by Ben Katarzynski

How May I Direct Your Call?

Once, in the aftermath of a snowstorm, my neighbor warned me about a downed power line in front of our apartment building. I lived in Maine and was working as a phone operator in a hospital at the time, and in between fielding phone calls and reciting a scripted greeting, I glanced at the text from my neighbor and wondered how effectively electricity traveled through snow, if at all. It was a real live wire. Would the rubber soles of my boots protect me?

A woman cried in my ear. Her name was Debra and a heart attack had crumpled her husband into a tidy shape for the EMTs to cart away. Debra's husband was forty-five and named Agate Hartmann. I was ten years younger than Agate, which was still old enough to speculate about my own death in a tangible way—the when and where and how of it all—but always the images in my mind unspooled in an alarming and infinite schema that was difficult to grasp. Too many possibilities existed.

Debra wanted to know where her husband was, so I transferred her call to a nurse. When in doubt, ask a nurse, although on the question of my own longevity I had no nurse to ask, and a part of me believed that I had made a biological and existential failure in being unable to pinpoint my own demise—I could say if I felt unwell or tired or hungry or sad or happy, but I doubted I would ever be able to say I felt dead.

I had failed in other more material ways as well. I sat in a chair with poor lumbar support and stared at a computer screen that displayed a spreadsheet of names and hospital bed numbers. I was never sure how much money I made an hour, receiving a base pay rate and differentials depending on whether I worked a morning, an evening, a weekday, a weekend, or a minor or major holiday. Math was not my strong suit. I was hungover and a college dropout—the loans were in default, the degree uncompleted, and I had a headache.

A coworker, Charlie, sat nearby, older than me and bearing the mechanical failures of death's impending approach—mysterious stomach ailments, remitted cancers, rusty joints, and a patchwork of scars indicative of surgeries designed to extend her life with metal and the harvested components of cadavers.

Charlie clutched her belly. A scar sickled her neck.

"Got a bellyache," she said, but not to me in particular. Just aloud. This was another aspect of aging and dying I had noticed: complaints were cast forth as if the world were a wishing well with the potential for transformative, pain-lessening power.

"It was probably that pineapple cottage cheese you found in the fridge," I said.

"What?"

"Your stomach."

"I wasn't talking to you."

And then a noise, a groan in a blender. I shrugged. Charlie had a past life, an older career now foundered—she was a former beauty queen of Maine. She still held the poise of a stage performer when she tapped her way through the halls of the hospital, beaming her smile at RNs and MDs and CNAs and CSRs. She had that sparkle and a set of partial dentures. It was hard for me to imagine making it so far in life.

Above my head a strip of windows provided a narrow view of the opposing building and, if I craned my neck, the hospital helipad. The office was dim, off-white, and lifeless, and I would call it portentous, if not for the commonplace reality of death's bureaucratic leanings—it whispered in my ear each day with phone calls from funeral parlors requesting corpses and phone calls from the banal voices of the bereaved wondering where their loved one's jewelry and clothes had been stashed.

Debra called again, except her crying had ceased.

"Where is my husband? I need to know where my husband is."

I pressed CTRL+H on the keyboard. That was my main function at work. Hot keys. His name appeared on the spreadsheet.

"He's in the Cath Lab." I didn't know what the Cath Lab was, exactly—Charlie told me it's where they put stents in hearts, but I didn't know what that meant either, just that I couldn't connect phone calls down there. An unreachable realm. I didn't even know if it was accurate for me to say "down there." The Cath Lab could have been above me. There were many floors and wings in the hospital.

"Let me talk to someone," Debra said.

"Unfortunately, because of where your husband is located, I can't connect your call. But once he's admitted to a room, we'll be able to connect you with the nurses on his floor."

"I want to speak to my husband. Or someone taking care of my husband."

"Unfortunately, because of where your husband is located, I can't connect your call."

"My husband."

"Unfor—"

Debra hung up. My neighbor still hadn't responded about the downed power line. And after I had agreed to watch his cat over the holidays. I was concerned for my safety and I wanted reassurance, so I searched online for an old PSA of some renown in Maine.

Created by Central Maine Power, the short film features two children possessed with the sort of impossible idiocy that amplifies the drama of their predicament with electricity. (I always hoped that the children in PSAs would learn how to ingest drugs properly and avoid strangers, but instead I—and every other viewer—bore witness to the terminus of their stupidity.) In the ad, their kite becomes entangled in a power line while a voice-over reminds the viewer that electrical lines can be charged with over three hundred thousand volts of electricity. A towheaded child begins to ascend a tree to retrieve his kite and meet death, and the camera cuts away to a lineman, a sort of urtext for dad bods—mustachioed and dressed in denim, all rural swagger and paternalism when he unrolls the thick poetry of his Maine accent: "And remembah, no line is safe to touch evah."

Here was a concrete, workable piece of knowledge: if encountered, do not touch a power line.

I watched the ad while the phone chimed in my ear. Debra again. Had anyone ever had a sexual awakening while watching that PSA? Debra was angry. Debra kept repeating herself.

"Transfer me to the Cat Lab."

"Cath Lab."

"What?"

"Your husband is in the Cath Lab."

"That's what I said. Transfer me to the Cath Lab. Why won't you transfer me? Is my husband dead? Are you telling me my husband is dead?"

"No, he's here."

This was true: dead people didn't appear on my spreadsheet. The morgue and the security office handled the corpses. The security officers were all amiable folks and not at all like the aggressive dilettantes of law and order one finds in malls and bank lobbies.

"Why won't you let me speak to my husband? How would you like it if your father was rushed to the hospital? I hope that never happens to you. I hope this never happens to you."

This was a common tactic, invoking my own loved ones. Of course, callers never knew the state of my loved ones.

"Please hold. Let me see what I can do."

With Debra on hold, I turned to Charlie.

"This woman won't shut up about the Cath Lab. She thinks her husband is dead."

"He's not dead. My friend has had five heart attacks and they just kept jamming stents in there." Charlie made a ring with her thumb and finger and mimed shoving stents into an aorta. "I keep telling him to quit smoking. There's a customer service desk in that area but I doubt anyone will answer. Send her there."

Charlie recited the number and I retrieved Debra from hold and transferred her call to a dead end. Presumably, Debra would call me back some time later, and I would assuage her anger and say, let's try that again, and transfer her to the same untended corner of the hospital. Some people can't accept no as an answer, and rather than spin in circles with them, I opted to allow them to spin alone, freely, at their own speed.

I texted my neighbor: Any flashing lights outside? Any dead squirrels on the ground, ha ha ha? But no response.

"I've never had a stent. Probably because of my life as a dancer. You should have seen my legs. One lady called them 'real gams.' They still said that kind of thing back then. I mean, she was old at the time. I'm not that old. My knees are old though. My knees are a real bitch."

Charlie hummed a tune while her feet tapped a rhythm beneath her desk.

I stood and paced the room, which only took three steps. On the rear wall was a window that overlooked the emergency room entrance, and I sometimes watched people arrive in various states of distress and deconstruction, but the entrance was empty now besides a valet parking attendant who leaned against a brick wall, waiting. The sun was setting when Debra called again.

"No one answered," she said.

My chair wheezed as I sat back down.

"I'm sorry. Let me see what else I can do." Whenever I said this, I paused for longer than necessary because I had few options but wanted to provide the illusion of effort. People favored the illusion of effort. It meant someone was trying, and it's not that I didn't care, but I simply lacked the resources to help.

I cleared my throat.

"Unfortunately, because of where your husband is located, I can't connect your call. But once he's admitted to a room, we'll be able to connect you with the nurses on his floor."

And then Debra started yelling. She called me useless, etc., but there seems little point in reciting her insults: they were hurtful in some way, but also boring. The average irate caller was prone to relying on the sturdy, familiar cairns of vulgarity, and I only ever encountered an occasional trailblazer, like the gentleman who called me a "dick licker." It was poetic, although maybe it was a stolen line. How would I know?

"I want to talk to the president."

"I can't connect you to the president."

I wasn't even sure who the president was. "Someone in administration then."

"If you want to make a complaint then I—"

"Yeah, I want to make a goddamn complaint."

I transferred her to Patient Matters, another phone tree and answering service that would return her call at the earliest possible convenience after they had sorted through their backlog.

The evening loped along. Most of the calls consisted of a scripted routine and the recitation of patient names and pleases and thank yous. Charlie hummed and groaned while my neighbor still neglected to text me. I queried the internet: will the rubber soles of my boots protect me from electrocution?

Answer: No, the sole is too thin and not of the right substance.

Anyone was old enough to die in a freak accident.

I said goodbye to Charlie. Charlie said goodbye to me.

For the most part, the night outside was calm. A few flakes whirled overhead, and lights flashed in the distance as plows scraped across the pavement. The snow and salt crunched beneath my feet, and streetlamps bathed the ground in spirals of light, making the snow glitter, and my breath came out in scoops while the cold air seeped into the soles of my boots.

I shivered and shrank and thought of the downed line. Soon I would be home. Still no response from my neighbor.

I arrived at the corner of my street and shuffled forward. Near my door was the downed line, coiled, its head writhing with a tongue of sparks. As I approached, a tremor whipped down the length of the line, and it turned and rose, a snake on its belly. It stared at me and canted its head. I waved and the head of the downed line traced my movements. Electric spurs fell from its mouth and pocked the snow with a hiss.

"I'm scared," I said to no one in particular, hoping my words would have some effect in the voicing. "I'm alone."

Mumbai, 2003

why the door to the garage can feel like a portal,
if only for the concrete waiting at the step, and

how sitting in this car alone in November can remind
and return you to a year you have already lived,

brings with it strange data, strings of memory you
can't do anything with, like call back the landlord

of that apartment you left, or work up the courage
to ask if she'll sign your yearbook after class,

I know how the fog retreats in the driveway and why
when you back out, it can feel like a film but no one

is watching except maybe the streetlights, or a neighbor
half-asleep by a window, her head rested on the glass,

husband snoring in rhythm, and the beam lights of your
car, dipping across the night, take her with you,

to somewhere the weather calls out like a horn,
somewhere to place the things you can't do anything with,

can you hear them in the garage, did you forget where
to go, *I am here, don't forget me, don't forget to*

take me home

Bad Acting: The Many Dark Revelations in *Tales the Devil Told Me*

Jen Fawkes. *Tales the Devil Told Me*. Winston-Salem, NC: Press 53, 2021. Pp. 196. $17.95. Softcover.

A villain will do most anything for the story. They will persuade. They will plot. They will continuously sulk and bemoan their loneliness. If provoked, they will growl at you like a wild animal or gobble you up in a pastry, or both. They will seek comfort, companionship. They will see ghosts. A villain will occasionally attempt to make amends for the wrongs they've done. And—perhaps most crucially—they will fail to make amends. Oftentimes, they will look up at you from the page with an anguished expression, their mouth full of declarations of love for the very being(s) they are forcibly depriving of life. Because a villain will not be—cannot be—the hero of the story, try as they might. But Jen Fawkes has no particular interest in heroics anyway. What the author's latest collection *Tales the Devil Told Me* offers, rather, is a fearsome yet accessible look at how these well-known antagonists may live with themselves when it proves next to impossible for anyone else to.

The opening story, "Demerol, Demerol, Benzedrine, Schnapps," presents a version of the Rumpelstiltskin tale rooted in the linguistic buoyancy of the Brothers Grimm. But in Fawkes' world, fantastical imagery is muddled by the paraphernalia of a disillusioned, America-adjacent society: "In front of his cottage, the rumpelstilt drank Kentucky bourbon whiskey, danced around the fire, and plotted. The world was teeming with cast-off human young—this he knew—but he did not want just any child" (1). Fawkes emphasizes here and elsewhere a quality in the so-called rumpelstilt not previously given much nuance: his isolation and his keen awareness of it, his longing for love, his coping mechanisms. The revisionist character is written as empathetic, seeing a stilted reflection of himself in the young woman whose baby it is he wants to embrace as his own. That you begin to wonder how it will end is a testament to the masterful way in which Fawkes works the aged fable into a frenzy of so many new emotions. And each story thereafter urges you to doubt your senses a little more and a little more.

One of *Devil*'s longest, most ambitious retellings is a subversive model of how to play with perspective. In "The Tragedie of Claudius, Prince of Denmark," Fawkes strips away the oft-rationalized motivations of Shakespeare's *Hamlet* to reveal an origin story that rivals its predecessor in patriarchal complications and moral convictions: "Wobbling on new legs, he advanced on Claudius, who inhaled sharply, for in that moment, the gosling seemed possessed—driven—as though he were animated by the spirit of a man rather than a beast, as though his ebony eyes were full of mad accusations" (58). For the first three odd acts—this tale indeed follows a classic five-act dramatic structure—Fawkes builds a kind of preface haunted by the peculiarities of its source material while excavating the possible inner life of a character usually only denoted as a murderous traitor. And, again, the alternative narration here isn't so much contesting that portrayal as it is engaging with what it means to become "convinced that [Claudius] rehearsed these actions a thousand times and could perform them without benefit of sight" (96) and "that he should take a moment before enacting his own death scene to deliver an internal soliloquy" (98). By allowing Claudius to grow increasingly aware of the fourth wall, Fawkes shifts attention from the finality of his deeds to the beauty of his mind. The depth of his consciousness is beautiful. Fawkes seems to recognize—and invites you to recognize in her elegiac prose—the near-redemptive power of knowing yourself.

As for the adult Mowgli in "Tigers Don't Apologize," Fawkes reshapes Rudyard Kipling's man-cub from *The Jungle Book* into a family man who is deeply ashamed of his animalistic tendencies, and that of his wife and young son. Because Mowgli historically exists inside a certain literary construct of British imperialism, it requires a bold author indeed to consign him to the eccentricities of modern suburban life: "Akela had been a fine leader of wolves, but in truth, Mowgli had never been more than a mediocre manager of pharmaceutical salesmen" (140-141). Evocative of a George Saunders protagonist, Fawkes' Mowgli is someone not at home in himself or anywhere else. The language she uses to draw out his consciousness is so dense with agony that you might fail to see the humor at first. But like the man-cub's true nature, Fawkes' humor only intensifies as things fall apart.

The twelve stories in *Tales the Devil Told Me* may sometimes remind you of love letters to characters who are—even here—indefensible. That is part of their allure. Fawkes' villains (or anti-heroes, if you prefer) are not willing or able to curb the impulses that leave them lonely. But they are rich in humanity as a result. These souls are weak and grotesque, splendid and grand. They may remind you of yourself. They may hold you and not let go. Thank goodness Fawkes' stories are stunning and mercurial enough to keep you wanting more.

Writing Through the Impossible: Sadie Hoagland's *Strange Children*

Sadie Hoagland. *Strange Children*. Pasadena, CA: Red Hen Press, 2021. Pp. 320. $17.95. Softcover.

Sadie Hoagland's story "Extra Patriotic" was published in SCR 51.2.

Listen. This is the first word of *Strange Children*—appropriate for a book we can hear, taste, smell, and touch as much as read. *Listen*, our mystery voice commands us, omniscient and foreboding: "I am the ghost of the dead girl. I have come to Redfield to watch the end come as the beginning." In *Strange Children*, we listen to the voices of children raised in a polygamist community and one ghost (also a child, for the record). And what we hear is both shocking and inevitable, a testament to how much Hoagland manages to pull off in the novel.

Twelve-year-old Emma and 16-year-old Jeremiah fall in love, or something like it, ("the light in me was God's love, and I was supposed to share it with Jeremiah," Emma swoons), and have sex, the catalyst for Redfield's downward spiral—although I think every reader can agree that any community whose mission includes men raping children in the name of God is hurtling toward an ugly end from conception. The nature of the story requires us to understand the children as adults, to recognize the very adult pressures placed upon them by Redfield. They are just as capable of damage as they are capable of being damaged. But in a system in which children and women, even men to a degree, are powerless before the will of God, who is culpable?

And while these children are certainly victims of Redfield, they also *are* Redfield, believing in and enacting the prophet's interpretation of God and justice to varying degrees.

To know these characters, to empathize, to love them—and I did—we must believe in it too. To read as an educated spectator who lives in the modern world with one partner and zero fear of God is to miss the point. It is to condemn without empathy. The book forces us to reexamine what makes something right. Is it not our belief that something is right?

Of course, we can't argue that murder and rape are right—that they are anything but horrifying. And Hoagland doesn't ask us to. The scene in which Jeremiah shoots and attempts to rape ex-girlfriend Haley, our omniscient ghost, as she bleeds out is indeed horrifying, and yet it is a scene I've gone back to again and again. Not because it's remotely pleasant to read. It's not. But it is a class in writing through the impossible. We are reeled so closely into Jeremiah's psyche and convinced that something impossible is also inevitable. While we can never forget the vile nature of the crime, Hoagland requires that we totally forget ourselves.

She does this through incredible language, fluid and slipping through time and fields of thinking. No surprise—the language throughout the novel does so much work to create a palpable, visual world inhabited by complex, flawed, and fully realized characters—but here, the language unravels into something capable of portraying Jeremiah's agony and wretched certainty of his own correctness: "He opened his mouth to scream but then he felt the gun in his hand. Substantial and sure in all this melting air, this watery brightness. The trigger a lighter. *Flick*. Like when she lit his first cigarette the day he met her. *Flick*."

This slippery, abstract language does more work to reveal Jeremiah's internal complexities and machinations than anything literal could have. To be in Jeremiah's point of view in this moment does ask a lot of us. We see his immediate regret upon shooting her, are reminded of his early understandings of spilling sinners' blood to help them atone for their earthly sins, and we see his warped, drugged-out justification of his own actions as having been done for her:

> But he couldn't let her back there without him. He had to be with her. To show her. To teach her. To protect her. He had to be with her. He pulled his knife from his pocket and opened it, gripping the blade with his palm....

> He had to be with her. How to get with her? He saw her skirt had come up. A black skirt. Slutty, he would've teased her. He unbuttoned his pants.

> This would be it. Emma was right. All this time she was right. He could feel what she'd said: *God's light in you telling you what you are supposed to do which is powerful and strange like and makes you do things you usually would not do. So this was the way to be together in God's light and the eternal Celestial heaven…"*

Yet Hoagland's reminder of the other partygoers watching this is a relief, grounding us in how truly horrific this is outside of Jeremiah's head. Without this, we just might believe that he will help her, protect her. Though of course we don't.

The language, mirroring that of Emma in the beginning of the book, reminds us of God, at the center of it all. Ironically, the most "God-like" character in the book is our ghost, Haley. *Listen*, she commands us, raising singing angels to mind. Her voice acts to build tension and warn us of what is to come, the only character with a bird's-eye view over everything. How wonderful when this all-knowing voice is revealed to belong to a 16-year-old girl, as far from the prophet's understanding of God as possible. By the end, she is more than a voice speaking to us, she is a puppet master pulling the characters' strings. Well deserved, after what this community did to her.

After the murder, Haley's mom says she doesn't blame Jeremiah but Redfield "at what they did to him." This is an easy and not incorrect justification. Of course Redfield is to blame. The crime is communal, the fault of everyone who touched Jeremiah as he walked down the path toward this nauseating, inevitable crime. And Jeremiah was a child—abused and left for dead. But even this isn't so straightforward. For what is Redfield if not people trapped, seemingly willingly (whatever willingly can mean when eternal damnation is on the line) under the same system of abuse.

One could argue the Prophet is to blame, and I'd say this is largely true. But even though he is the most powerful character of the book—the voice of God, a rapist, an accomplice to murder, a cruel man—through Haley, we see moments of his powerlessness too: "I saw you Prophet on your knees. Asking, asking, squeezing your hands together as if to hold water." And as we watch Emma become Savior Angel, we see how easy it is for even a child to become warped by power and a genuine belief in her own holy goodness. So who is to blame, then? Who is to blame when everyone feels they are doing what is right in the eyes of God, but what is "right" is most certainly wrong? When the rules are flawed, who is responsible for the havoc wreaked when they are followed?

Strange Children asks big, uncomfortable questions of the reader—questions about religion, blame, abuse, pedophilia, morality, want, death. But alongside it all, the layers of right and wrong within each character's narrow understanding of the world and their place in it, is a simple, quiet love of place and people. Yes, there is fear and pain that can't even be verbalized as wrong, so enmeshed is it in God's will: Annalue's desire to cleanse her body in the creek after the Prophet rapes her; Levi's desire to steal the truck and run away to the town for the morning; Manti's desire to burn the Prophet's house down. But there is also beauty within the pain.

This love exists within every point of view character, even in those who have left or those who wish to, like Annalue:

If I remember the place when I am asleep, it is not just the whole earth but also the whole world again. The world as it was for years and that is this: My hand over Emma's smaller one, teaching her to milk, squeezing the hot gray teat through her fingers to show her the pressure, the pulling motion, her cry that I am crushing her fingers, the cow stamping away flies, and the milk finally sounding in the pail.

That's all it is."

The strange children of Redfield proved themselves capable of murder, deception, and arson, but in moments like the above, we recognize them as people, moving forward as they can, finding glory in the ordinary. Are they so different from us?

"A woman can make a living": Heather Herrman's *The Corpse Queen*

Heather Herrman. *The Corpse Queen*. New York: Penguin Teen, 2021. Pp. 416. $18.99. Hardcover.

Heather Herrman's story "Monsoon" was published in SCR *38:2.*

Seventeen-year-old Molly Green has lived in a church orphanage for nearly four years when her best friend, Kitty, dies under mysterious circumstances. Our opening scene? Molly cradling the mutilated corpse, a girl left rotting in a river by the nuns who raised her.

Hold tight, readers: Heather Herrman's *The Corpse Queen* (Penguin Teen, 2021) is just getting started.

Mother Superior uses Molly's interference with the body as an excuse to give her the boot, resigning the fiercely independent teen to a mysterious (and wealthy) aunt conveniently emerged from the woodwork. "Leave the shoes," says Mother Superior, and Molly climbs atop the waiting carriage with rags donning her feet. Convinced her parents died with no siblings, Molly is naturally suspicious of Ava Green, her new relative in question. When dear Aunt Ava insists Molly fund her plush new living arrangements by joining a massive grave robbing operation, her suspicions are confirmed.

Herrman's feminist horror story plays with Gothic tradition in its sumptuous aesthetic (the novel is set in 1850s Philadelphia) and unflinching focus on death and dying. Lines such as "Statues flanked the path like corpses, their marble bodies twisted into unnatural shapes," describing Ava's estate, frequently play with the intersection of landscape and fear. She clutches you in the opening chapters, with plenty of guts and gore to go around, as Molly begins her journey in body snatching. However, as the novel continues, it becomes clear that our heroine refuses to be anything resembling a Gothic victim of circumstance.

Molly secretly manipulates her position as a grave robbing apprentice to pursue the serial killer known as Knifeman, whom she deems responsible for Kitty's death (as well as the gruesome deaths of dozens of other young women). But as Molly delves deeper into this dark world, she recognizes an even larger villain at play. Despite the palpable horror constructed around Knifeman's murders, Herrman's language is unequivocal that society is truly Molly's greatest threat. Philadelphia is haunted by a patriarchy that tyrannizes and ruins the bodies of women alive, dead, and—more often than not—in the dangerous space between those two poles.

In her own words, Molly just "wanted to be allowed to want," to make her own choices about the future. At first, grave robbing at least seems like the best-worst opportunity for a woman in this town, until Molly learns the decomposing bodies she gathers from bars, cemeteries, and homes often end up with the prominent Dr. Lavalle, host of controversial and secretive lectures that explore and manipulate the human form. It is by finally sneaking into one of these lectures, held on Ava Green's property, that Molly finds herself enamored with the male-centered world of anatomy and medicine. Bodies, even days after death, continue to heal and create life—but is this man's world ready for a woman to take the knife? As the book progresses, I find myself less afraid of Molly being attacked by a serial killer and more afraid of Molly being held from her potential. Female ambition, in turn, becomes *The Corpse Queen*'s cornerstone.

Using an effective limited third-person narration, Herrman shows us Molly's personal growth not only through her actions but in how she describes bodies. Her figurative language regarding corpses slowly shifts from the gag-inducing (see: "potted meat left in the sun") to the more reverent and precious ("small dark flecks of beard, which looked like pencil shavings against the parchment of his skin"). Molly's understanding of the human form and its power matures by the sentence, as she slowly learns to see bodies as more than parts to be gathered and sold. But what of the bodies still breathing, even barely so? As Molly herself thinks: "The tenuous flame of life was not so very much to separate the living from the dead."

One of Herrman's greatest strengths in *The Corpse Queen* is her wealth of complex female characters and their diverse relationships with the living body. Throughout the book, we meet people who see flesh as transaction, as sacrifice, as power. Ginny, a performer and sex worker at the Red Carousel, stands out as a particularly vibrant character. After Molly discovers her with a client, Ginny snaps: "at least it's my *own* body I sell [...] which one of us is disgusting?" I am reminded of how our capitalist society actively shames women who earn a living with their own bodies, but has no problem commodifying the female form for its own institutional benefit. While surrounding us with cadavers and killers, Herrman somehow turns our gaze, again and again, towards subtle horrors beneath the surface, the ones that have lingered among us for generations.

When Molly first arrives at the Corpse Queen's mansion, Ava Green explains: "A body is the only way a woman can make a living in this world. I just choose not to use my own." In some ways, Herrman does the same, crafting a book full of bodies laid bare for readers to explore and savor.

Unlearning Shame: *Mother Body* by Diamond Forde

Diamond Forde. *Mother Body*. Philadelphia: Saturnalia Books, 2021. Pp. 80. $16.00. Softcover.

Diamond Forde's poetry appeared in SCR *54.1.*

In *Mother Body,* Diamond Forde's poems sing the personal political and reclaim agency and joy in a fat, Black, and femme body. She writes in defiance of the looming patriarchal specters of attacks on women's rights to make decisions about their bodies and health, of years of countless attacks on Black bodies from police who are theoretically there to protect them, and of the constant intrusions of diet culture and westernized beauty standards that devalue bodies of size and bodies of color—and, moreover, bodies that dare to exist despite not fitting into the tidy mold of the white male gaze's definition of what constitutes a body worthy of adoration, protection, and self-governance. Forde's speaker seeks to decolonize the fat, Black, and femme body by interrogating the labels and narratives that have been thrust upon her. *Mother Body* is, at its core, an exploration of how shame is learned and what it takes to unlearn shame.

The book consists of a proem, "Blood Ode,"† followed by three untitled sections that are separated by illustrations from Diana Kitthajaroenchai. "Blood Ode" introduces a recurring character, "Fat Girl." Upon cutting herself while shaving, "Fat Girl" beholds the trickle of blood and views it as a "worthless currency" that "cannot buy a country but becomes it" (3–4). The sight of the blood spawns her meditation on the ways that the blood of Black bodies has been treated as worthless:

> ...fat girl weeps
> for the blood that won't return—
> how many mothers have tried

such a homecoming, sons and daughters
inking the tarry streets? (5–9)

Here, Forde summons up the too-common images of police brutality, of bodies "inking the tarry streets" with their "blood that won't return." Notably, the poet has dedicated this poem to "Breonna Taylor, George Floyd, Ahmaud Arbery, and the numerous, numerous Black lives lost to police brutality." The poem turns to reflect on how growing up with the normalization of these brutal images has affected "Fat Girl." In an homage to poet Angel Nafis, Forde writes,

    …fat girl becomes
a mother through her looking, has seen
too many children mangled by a sense
of justice. She carries somebody's child
in the crater their deaths create
inside her. (9–14)

We are told that seeing all of these images of brutalized Black bodies has turned the "Fat Girl" into a mother, which is an important definition of motherhood: to be a mother (and perhaps, more specifically, a Black mother) is being defined as a state of worry, a state of wanting to "make a bulletproof lung" (17), of wanting to fashion a new mode of survival in a society bent on killing Black children.

The first main section of *Mother Body* consists of poems that primarily detail the speaker's changing relationship to her body during adolescence, meditating on moments when the speaker was taught to view her body as shameful or unworthy. For instance, in the prose poem "The Last Time You Are Close to Your Body," the speaker's stepmother tells her that she is "disgusting" for scrubbing her undergarments in the bathroom sink, as she had been taught to do by an aunt when her family was "too poor for hygiene." The poem ends with the speaker reflecting upon an image of her mother in a "ratty blue bathrobe" and concluding that the stepmother, who comes from a more affluent background, "would never touch anything that feels like poverty on the palms—she will never hold you [the speaker]." Other poems in this section include a blond classmate telling her to shave her arms ("Three Lessons on the Adolescent Body") and her ailing grandfather saying he is glad she isn't "fat yet" ("The Last Time I Saw My Grandfather"). The section concludes with "Ode to Magic," a poem about how the speaker learned her body could be a form of currency, that it could get her things. In the poem, she acknowledges that her mother slept "beside a man /she didn't love" (16–17) and that a neighbor boy picked her flowers for "the chance to rest his hand on the copper / pennies of [her] brown, growing breasts (20–21). It is a poem about a girl learning to value her body based on what it can inspire men to do, rather than viewing it as inherently valuable and worthy.

The second section of the book begins with the speaker's inability to achieve self-love ("There's No Praise in Me for Me") and builds toward the speaker developing a sense of awe and reverence for her body ("Ode to My Stomach"). In "Ode to My Stomach," the speaker marvels at her body's unsung mechanics:

> I do not know how many miles
> you hold inside you, the intestinal road
> my dinner travels even now,
> down the muscular clutch waking
> like proofed dough.
> …
>   You are
> honey dome. Power house. Piston
> of digestion pump-pumping. You roar
> with need or function. (1–5, 7–10)

In this section, the speaker also reveals how pain complicates her relationship with her body. Her poem "What I Have to Give" describes the event of a pelvic exam in which the speaker understates the level of menstrual pain she experiences while talking to the gynecologist. Of the many impressive aspects of this book, I am particularly floored by the clarity of image in the opening stanza of this poem: "The speculum, spread apart / like knees, opens / a curtain off my cervix cinema" (1–3). I would like to argue for more speculums and cervixes in poems; too often women's bodies are rewritten as shameful by the silences that surround them. Forde's voice here is unabashed in claiming that women's lives (and bodies) are the stuff of poetry. Her poem "Hysterectomy" is another power-house, in which the speaker contemplates a hysterectomy in order to alleviate her extreme menstrual pain, but other people (her doctor, her mother, etc.) argue that she should not complete the procedure because she "*might want kids one day*" (11). Poignantly, the speaker remarks on how it difficult it is "not to be defined by motherhood" (9), highlighting the societal expectation that having a uterus means one should want to grow a baby inside of it, even if that uterus causes unmanageable pain.

Many of the poems in the final section of this collection return to the "Fat Girl" character introduced in the proem "Blood Ode". The section's first poem, "Fat Fuck," interrogates derogatory names the speaker has been given for her body: "fat fuck. moose knuckle. /

flabby ass. cankles" (31–32) and presents a speaker who is fed up with fat-shaming rhetoric. This section's reclaiming of the body begins with necessary, well-earned anger at those who have devalued the speaker's body and ebbs into self-love, embracing her sexuality, and even ordering a McFlurry from a drive-thru without shame. One of my favorite poems of this section, "Still Life with Fat Girl, Post-Coitus," reads like a love poem celebrating the erotic and beautiful body of the "Fat Girl" character. Again, the clarity of image the poem opens with is immediately grounding: "Spread over indigo light, sweat- / dimpled and satisfied, she basks / in amaretto aftermath" (1–3). While a number of the poems in the collection describe "Fat Girl's" body through a negative light, this poem looks at it basking in mood lighting, as it "sweat- / dimpled and satisfied." The poem is celebratory and tender in its descriptions:

> ...her thighs
>
> circle her sex like a bowl of fruit. Look
> how the lacework from her lingerie paints
>
> shadows: incandescent shards,
> or pinpoints of light, and embroidery
>
> of sequins in her sweat. (16–21)

The woman described is clearly a woman who wants to be seen, which is a marked transformation from the beginning of the collection: "She will not apologize / for the animal she's become / for once" (26–28). I have talked quite a bit about the clarity of Forde's imagery, but I think it would be remiss not to mention her remarkable poetic ear. I swear that Diamond Forde is the queen of consonance, among other things. There is such great pleasure in reading these poems aloud.

In terms of the journey toward self-love in this collection, it ends with a scene of self-pleasure in "Fat Girl Climaxes While Working Out at the Gym." In this poem, the speaker shouts to the rooftops about how much she loves her body: "I want / my pussy to know I have loved it since the first time / I pried its smile into a lazy camera's eye, / spied its abundance of pink" (11–14). The poem (and collection) concludes with the speaker's sexual climax: "Pussy, we are loud / with an insistence to be. We are a nailbed cupped / with cum, a scuffle of air hoping to lung" (32–34). This insistence on loudness, on taking up space, on seeing the body as a site of pleasure and not shame, demonstrates the speaker's move toward unity with her body. Throughout much of the collection, the speaker is at odds with her body and other people's reactions to it, but here she is (quite literally) embracing herself.

Rather serendipitously, I have found myself reading *Mother Body* on the day after the US Supreme Court chose not to strike down Texas's highly restrictive abortion law—it is the book I need for facing this day. I am grateful for the loudness of the poems in *Mother Body*. Forde's poems are equal parts intimate and audacious, tender and ferocious, elegant and bawdy—and I am one hundred percent here for it. The speaker in these poems owns every inch of herself, and in a world that persistently encroaches on women's agency over their bodies, such loudness is precious and necessary. As a white woman, I cannot speak with authority about the inheritance of our country's centuries of systemically disenfranchising the bodies of Black women, but I am grateful to Forde for allowing this vulnerable glimpse into the chorus of voices that devalue the bodies of women. Diamond Forde's *Mother Body* feels overwhelmingly prescient as America, once again, reminds us that the bodies of women—especially Black women, especially Black women of size—remain a contested political ground.

Deception, Guilt, and the Search for Racial Redemption in Marlin Barton's *Children of Dust*

Marlin Barton. *Children of Dust*. Raleigh, NC: Regal House Publishing, 2021. Pp. 298. $16.95. Softcover.

Marlin Barton's story "Up a River" was published in SCR *54.1.*

In Robert Frost's "Home Burial," a dramatic monologue published in *North of Boston* (1915), a husband and wife are at the breaking point in their marriage following the death of their infant child. The husband, who has just come in from burying the child himself in the small family graveyard near their home, finds his wife looking at the child's mound from an upstairs window. Each does not know how to cope with the loss. She is angry that he seems to treat the burial so cavalierly, and he is frustrated that she will not let him mourn in his own way. Words are inadequate, and the couple no longer communicates except through hurt and accusations. When she threatens once again to leave, seeking solace from someone else, he cries out for her to help him understand her grief.

Though Barton does not acknowledge Frost as an influence, there are a number of parallels between the poem and his latest novel *Children of Dust*, among them the inability to share one another's grief and all of the misunderstandings between men and women that often lead to destruction. In a 2020 interview with *Water Stone Review*, Barton says that he often writes about grief and how his characters struggle to cope with it. Families torn apart by or living with fear and mistrust must somehow come together in this richly cultural and historical fictional narrative whose aim is to unite the past with the present and reconcile long-buried racial secrets. Like the couple in "Home Burial," Barton's protagonists often speak their own grief not *with* but *at* one another.

Marlin Barton was born in the Black Belt region of central Alabama on October 25, 1961, and now lives with his wife in a house overlooking the Alabama River in Montgomery. *Children of Dust* is his third novel, and he has also published three collections of short stories. His stories have appeared in such prominent Southern journals as *The Sewanee Review*, *Shenandoah*, *The Southern Review*, and *Virginia Quarterly Review*. He has been awarded an O. Henry prize (1994) and been featured in *Best American Short Stories* (2010). He has a BA from the University of Alabama and an MFA from Wichita State University. Since 1977, he has taught in the creative writing program for juveniles called "Writing Our Stories," created by the Alabama Writers' Forum. He also teaches at the low-residency MFA program at Converse College in Spartanburg, South Carolina.

Being raised in the Black Belt region gives Barton's fiction an authenticity and a connection with the historical events of the post-Civil War South that long have been the subject of questions of freedom, race, and multigenerational guilt. The central narrative of *Children of Dust* is set in the late 1880s in rural Alabama, but the story begins and ends with the points of view of two contemporary descendants of those turbulent days: Seth Anderson, who is white, and Charles Anderson, who is of mixed race. As their newfound friendship deepens and they recognize a shared biological history, each must come to terms with the brutality, racial and cultural prejudice, and misogyny of their ancestors.

In antebellum Alabama, Melinda Anderson is giving birth to her tenth child, a boy, and tended to by Annie Mae Posey, housekeeper and midwife. Melinda is married to Rafe, a hardened Civil War veteran who has seen four years of killing. The couple has previously lost four children before the age of three. Annie Mae lives in a nearby cabin with her light-skinned daughter Betsy (Elizabeth), who is brought to the house to take care of the newborn. The next morning, however, the child has died, and Rafe suspects that Annie Mae, who is part Choctaw, part Negro and schooled in the mysteries of the occult, has taken its breath. The child died before its naming ceremony, a Choctaw ritual, though Melinda calls him Jacob. She refuses to tell her husband that she named the child, partly out of respect to Annie Mae's abilities as midwife and partly to spite her husband for his many infidelities, including Betsy.

Rafe buries the child, not at the church cemetery, but at home, as he had done previously with the others. He also accuses his wife of hurting the child on purpose: "How did you let that child die?" (47). His suspicion only rivals Melinda's, who suspects Betsy killed it. As the story unfolds, we also learn that Rafe has two more children with Virginia, a former slave. Virginia, who is angry at Rafe's infrequent visits and minimal attention to the children, tells him that Melinda is punishing him for being with her. When Rafe returns home, Melinda, who knows about his second "family," tells him not to let "that girl" and her "bastard children" (62) into her home again.

As the novel unfolds, there are also flashbacks to when 15-year-old Rafe first came to Alabama from North Carolina after nearly beating another child to death, how he and 14-year-old Melinda first met, and how he repeatedly justifies that "dark part of himself" (56) in his selfish choices: "With women you did what you wanted, and the only instinct that mattered was desire" (56). Those choices will poison not only his immediate family, but also his entire lineage, as is clearly shown in the ways his modern-day "children of dust," Seth and Charles, try to piece together a common thread of what each knows—however incomplete—about the family's racial violence, issues of mistrust, and cultural misunderstandings from over one hundred years ago. In one of the more poignant moments in the novel, Charles shows Seth an old box containing braids of Betsy's hair, cut from her by Rafe in a violent rage. Not wanting to "lose the connection" (294) of their common humanity, each takes one end of the braid: "For a moment neither of them let go, and neither attempts to pull away from the other" (295).

Marlin Barton is a gifted storyteller whose vivid style perfectly captures the time and place of the South following the Civil War. His characters are well-drawn, and his gritty realism has been compared to the works of Larry Brown and Ron Rash. In a 2005 interview for *Eclectica Magazine*, Barton acknowledges that a writer's job is to look at all parts of human nature, both good and evil. In *Children of Dust*, he shows how the choices we make reverberate far beyond the present. As Rafe himself muses early on in the novel, "Maybe God did work to make things balance" (18). Barton warns that not finding that equilibrium can cause generations of a family—and indeed, a whole cultural tradition—to fail.

The Future Feels Like This: Lance Olsen's *Skin Elegies*

Lance Olsen. *Skin Elegies*. Dzanc Books, 2021. Pp. 248. $16.95. Softcover.

An excerpt from Lance Olsen's novel My Red Heaven *was published in* SCR *50.2.*

I read this book on an airplane. Just before takeoff, I fished it out of a bag stuffed with crayons, cloth dolls, Cajun peanuts spilled from their plastic pouch, a small pair of socks, tangle of neon earbud wires, pages and pages of loose, dog-eared paper, another book, another book, an inexplicable spoon. My seven-year old was sitting beside me reading the laminated safety pamphlet and acting out the dramas therein in the sotto voce tone she reserves for reveries she doesn't want to have to explain. "Wheee," she whispered, "after the airplane crashes, we all get to float on a raft!" As the plane idled on the runway, I read the book's blurbs and back pages. As the plane swung toward the horizon, I flipped to the beginning and read the epigraphs from Merwin, Mark Strand, McCarthy, Hughie Charles. I paused to tighten my daughter's seatbelt and offer her some scattered peanuts from the bottom of my bag. The plane roared down the runway and tilted its nose to the sky. As we tugged reluctantly free of gravity, I read the first stuttering pages. In a tube where the hollow air popped in my sinuses, hurtling upward at impossible speeds, my daughter beside me who had once been inside me, the book in my hands pretending to be a sound in my ears which, soon, it became.

I know this is not how reviews start. It doesn't, and shouldn't, matter to the reader where I was when I read this book or who was next to me. But it does matter to me. Even if my experience isn't likely to be replicated—the reader may read this book in a bathtub, or at a bus station, in a clearing in the forest, or in bed late at night—the physical act of my engagement with this book was specific and precise and linked intimately with the project of *Skin Elegies,* which is to both take us out of ourselves and to make us more ourselves. So much ourselves that perhaps we just can't stand it. So much ourselves we may not survive.

The conceit behind *Skin Elegies* is scantily delineated. Rather, Olsen dives right into the meat of the matter, the synapses of the matter, the sparking neurons firing unraveling patterns of the matter. The year is 2072. An American couple—Josiah and Elisha Richardson, a neuroscientist and climatologist respectively who were reeducated to work in the Evangelical Bank in New Jerusalem under the Reformation Government—have been evacuated by the American Resistance in an attempt to avoid their public crucifixion. They have made their way to the Mind Emulation Studies Department at Cairo University where, motivated by a desire to thwart global totalitarian efforts to erase all cultural memories that don't support regime ideology, they have volunteered to become the first human subjects to have their consciousness fully digitized in the Refugee Mind Upload Project. "Three, two, one, and…," says Dr. Arafa, the chair of the program, as she flips the switch that will zap them into binary code. But all this happens at the end of the book. At the beginning, page one, two, three, four, five as the plane pierced the cloud bank and my daughter kicked the seat back in front of her, all the reader sees are the disassociated pixels of Josiah and Elisha's thoughts. "I—I—I—I—I—I—," says page four. "Don't do that," I said to my daughter.

From these pixilated beginnings, we flash immediately into spasms of narrative. Each section, some no longer than a sentence, features a different narrative figure and context carefully delineated by time stamp. Each is situationally unlike the one that has come before but empathetically similar. Humans are speaking. Humans are in extremum and are relating their distress. Humans are remembering things that should never have had to be said or envisioning the act of changing the future in its totality for everyone who came after. I penciled in the dates on the back pages of the book. "I thought you said not to write in books," said my daughter, who was using my phone to take pictures of the airplane's shadow stenciled across the clouds below. "It's ok to write in this book," I told her. "It's a hard book. You have to figure it out." But that wasn't quite right. The book isn't hard so much as it is heedless. Of the reader's expectations. Of the way books are supposed to be written. In 2011, we meet a young woman who survived the Fukushima tsunami by standing on the kitchen table in her parents' house as they drowned. She writes her story on her cell phone, the lines strictly controlled by the vertical linearity of her screen. In 1945, we look in on the deathbed interrogation of an SS officer fleeing the advancing Russian line in the final moments before he puts a bullet in his brain. In 1986, we are part of the meticulous science of the Challenger disaster as it ascends, falters, explodes, dives flaming into the sea. "What's below us right now, Mom?" my daughter asked. "The ocean, I think," I said. "Cool," she said. "Maybe we'll see a shark."

There are other stories interrupting each other here: David Sanders bleeds to death at Columbine in 1999; Mark David Chapman stalks John Lennon outside The Dakota in 1980; a young Syrian refugee is put on a raft by his father to cross the Mediterranean in 2015. Some of these are first person and some are framed narratives bounded by technologies we have not yet acquired here in 2021. In 1969, for example, on the day the internet is first switched on, the switch-flippers in question, Charley Kline and Bill Duvall, are interviewed from the future by Ry Himari, the host of Random Access Memory pod cast, who is as incredulous as everyone else that for Kline and Duvall it was just another day. Some of the sections are more or less anonymous: a daughter under the sway of her father's god complex enables his abuse of her mother in 1974; on September 11, 2001 a doctor in Switzerland assists an elderly woman in her medical suicide as in the background on a morning news show the Twin Towers fall. What these sections have in common is our sense of trespass. We are inside the moments where the self disassociates, the body scrambles, the great "I Am" becomes a particulate we, untethered from the fragile nexus of human identity, scattered into space between binaries—cyber space, atomic space.... it hardly matters. What does matter is that it is retrieved from the past by the means of a digitization that is both the conceit of the book and the fact of the book itself. That we can witness both the word and the space between the word. That we, like Josiah and Elisha, are somehow both the ghost in the machine and the machine itself. "That we are the machine," I write in the back of the book as my daughter, asleep beside me, rests her head on the crook of my elbow. Her hair is very long and blonde. It frays at the ends where she needs a haircut and I have to move carefully so as not to tug her hair where it catches between my arm and my body, tangles in the buttons of my shirt, nooses around one finger raised to turn the page.

In Lance Olsen's *Skin Elegies* what cannot be replicated is touch. In each section, a character reaches out a hand and finds emptiness at the other end. In each section, when touch comes again—the father enveloping his son in a hug in 2015, the doctor stroking his patient's forehead as she opens the IV valve to admit the poison in 2001—it reminds the reader of how completely we fill our bodies, no space left over, and makes us wonder when we leave our bodies behind at last what shape will suffice to contain us. "There is nothing, nothing whatsoever, that brings you into the present quite like letting go of someone's hand," says the SS officer as he recalls the seconds before he pulled the trigger on the gun he had pressed below his chin. "*Here it comes,*" the burning children whisper into Christa McAuliffe's burning mouth. "*Here it comes, the future, and it will always look exactly like this.*"

The plane began to descend, breaking again through the clouds. My daughter woke up and looked out the window. I finished the book and closed it, shoving it back into my bag. Into all the different worlds we had briefly left as we hurtled through the air (the ground obscured, the ground erased, the ground forgotten) my daughter and I returned just exactly the same as we were before in spite of our travels. A book doesn't change you, I thought, so much as it reminds you of the ways in which you are always changing. "Hold my hand," my daughter said as the wheels bumped down. "This is the scary part."

CONTRIBUTORS

TALAL ALYAN is a Palestinian-American writer based in Brooklyn. His debut collection of poetry, *Babeldom*, was published by Astrophil Press in 2019.

SUSAN AYRES is a poet, lawyer, and translator. She holds an MFA in creative writing with a concentration in translation from Vermont College of Fine Arts, and a PhD in literature from Texas Christian University. Her work has been nominated for a Pushcart Prize, and has appeared in many journals, including *Sycamore Review*, *Cimarron Review*, and *Valparaiso Review*. She lives in Fort Worth and teaches at Texas A&M University School of Law. She can be reached at https://psusanayres.com/.

When not teaching, **DEVON BALWIT** chases chickens and restocks her Little Free Library in Portland, Oregon. Her poems and reviews can be found in *The Worcester Review*, *The Cincinnati Review*, *Tampa Review*, *Barrow Street*, *Tar River Poetry*, *Sugar House Review*, *Rattle*, *Bellingham Review*, and *Grist* among others. Her most recent chapbook is *Rubbing Shoulders with the Greats* (Seven Kitchens Press, 2020). Her collection *Dog-walking in the Shadow of Pyongyang* is forthcoming (Nixes Mate Books, 2021) For more, please visit her website at: https://pelapdx.wixsite.com/devonbalwitpoet.

SARAH BLACKMAN is Director of Creative Writing at the Fine Arts Center, a magnet arts high school in Greenville, South Carolina. Her books, *Mother Box and Other Tales* and *Hex*, were published by FC2.

ADRIENNE K. BURRIS is a writer/teacher in Greenville, South Carolina, where she works with young authors at the Fine Arts Center. Her poetry can be found in *Washington Square Review*, *Rogue Agent Journal*, and *Kakalak*, among others.

BRIAN CLIFTON is the author of the chapbooks *MOT* and *Agape* (from Osmanthus Press). They have work in: *Pleiades, Guernica, Cincinnati Review, Salt Hill, Colorado Review, The Journal, Beloit Poetry Journal*, and other magazines. They are an avid record collector and curator of curiosities.

STEPHAN EIRIK CLARK is the author of the novel *Sweetness #9* and the story collection *Vladimir's Mustache*. A former Fulbright Fellow to Ukraine, he directs the MFA Program in Creative Writing at Augsburg University and lives in St. Paul with his Russian wife and three children.

BROCK CLARKE is the author of seven books of fiction, most recently a collection of short stories, *The Price of the Haircut*. He teaches creative writing at Bowdoin College.

ELI COYLE (he/him) received his MA in English from California State University-Chico, and is currently an MFA candidate at the University of Nevada-Reno. His poetry has recently been published or is forthcoming in: *New York Quarterly, Barely South Review, Camas, Tule Review, Caustic Frolic*, the *Cosumnes River Journal, Deep Wild*, the *Helix Magazine*, and elsewhere.

STEVIE EDWARDS holds a PhD in creative writing from University of North Texas and an MFA in poetry from Cornell University. Her poems are published and forthcoming in *Poetry Magazine, American Poetry Review, Missouri Review, Crazyhorse, Crab Orchard Review, BOAAT, The Adroit Journal*, and elsewhere. She is a Lecturer at Clemson University and author of *Sadness Workshop* (Button Poetry, 2018), *Humanly* (Small Doggies Press, 2015), and *Good Grief* (Write Bloody Publishing, 2012). She is the Senior Editor in Book Development at YesYes Books and served as the Founding Editor-in-Chief of *Muzzle Magazine* from 2010-2020. Originally a Michigander, she now lives in South Carolina with her husband and a small herd of rescue pitbulls (Daisy, Tinkerbell, and Peaches).

JUAN CAMILLO GARZA is a Mexican-American poet based in Austin, Texas. They have been at times a construction worker, clothing salesman, mascot, inflated bureaucrat, copywriter, and cook. Their writing can be found in *Columbia Journal, Poet Lore, Raleigh Review, The Oakland Review, Button Poetry, Hobart Pulp, Watershed Review, Allegory Ridge, Typishly*, and elsewhere.

ROBIN GOW is a trans and queer poet and YA author from and living in rural Pennsylvania. They are the author of *Our Lady of Perpetual Degeneracy* and the chapbook *Honeysuckle*. Their first YA novel, *A Million Quiet Revolutions*, is forthcoming with FSG Books for Young Readers.

K. IVER is a nonbinary poet born in Mississippi. Their work has appeared or is forthcoming in *BOAAT, Boston Review, Gulf Coast, Puerto del Sol*, and elsewhere.

ALEXIS IVY is a 2018 recipient of the Massachusetts Cultural Council Fellowship in Poetry and the author of *Romance with Small-Time Crooks* (BlazeVOX, 2013), and *Taking the Homeless Census* (Saturnalia Books, 2020) which won the 2018 Saturnalia Editors Prize. She is a 2021 Writing Fellow at the Rensing Center in Pickens, South Carolina. A native of Boston, she works as an advocate for the homeless and teaches in the PoemWorks community.

DARON JOHNSON is a current undergraduate student at the University of Nebraska-Lincoln whose work has been featured in *The Laurus Literary Magazine, Bayou Magazine*, and *Not Your Mother's Breast Milk*.

ANNA BLAKE KEELEY is a fiction editor at *quip lit review*. She holds an MFA from the University of North Carolina at Greensboro, where she was fiction editor of *The Greensboro Review*. She lives in Denver, Colorado, with her two dogs.

GARY KERLEY, PhD from the University of South Carolina, is retired and living in Bermuda Run, North Carolina. He has published extensively in journals and encyclopedias. A regular reviewer for *Publishers Weekly*, he has recent work in *James Dickey Review* and *The Southern Register*.

CINDY KING's work appears in *The Sun, Callaloo, Prairie Schooner, Crab Orchard Review, River Styx, Cincinnati Review, Gettysburg Review, North American Review*, and elsewhere. Her debut poetry collection, *Zoonotic*, is forthcoming (Tinderbox Editions, 2021). Her chapbook, *Easy Street*, was released by Dancing Girl Press in March 2021. Originally from Cleveland, Ohio, she currently lives in St. George, where she is an assistant professor of creative writing at Dixie State University and editor of *The Southern Quill*.

Poems by **PJ KRASS** have appeared in journals including *Adirondack Review, Rattle, Atlanta Review,* and *New Verse News*. He's received a Pushcart Prize special mention, and he teaches at The Writers Studio. PJ's chapbook *My Sixties* is forthcoming later this year.

KATE KRAUTKRAMER's work has appeared in such publications as *North American Review, Colorado Review, Fiction, Creative Nonfiction, National Geographic Magazine, Washington Square,* and the *New York Times* (Modern Love). She's been included in *The Beacon Best, The Best American Nonrequired Reading,* and *Best of the West* anthologies and has twice been nominated for a Pushcart Prize. She lives in rural Colorado with her husband and children.

EVAN J. MASSEY is an African-American, U.S. Army veteran who served his country in Afghanistan. His work can be found or is forthcoming in *The Pinch, Gulf Coast, The Rumpus, Willow Springs, Southern Indiana Review,* and others. He teaches Upper School English at The Rivers School.

MIRIAM MCEWEN writes about disability and bodily autonomy. She holds an MFA in Writing from Vermont College of Fine Arts. She is an associate editor at *The South Carolina Review* and a co-editor for *The Swamp*. Miriam's work has appeared or is forthcoming in *SAND Journal, Under the Gum Tree,* and *Madcap Review,* among others. She lives in the foothills of South Carolina.

LEILA ORTIZ is a poet and social worker born and raised in NYC. Her work has appeared in *Apogee, Sixth Finch, The Recluse, Tinderbox,* and *Anomaly,* among others. She has forthcoming work in *Até Mais,* an anthology of Latinx Futurisms. She is a graduate of the Queens College MFA Program in Creative Writing and Literary Translation.

ROMINA PAREDES holds a master's degree in audiovisual translation from Universitat Autònoma de Barcelona. She was a member of the Peruvian Swimming Team (2002, 2003) during her teens, and pursued college swimming until 23. She uses social media only to watch cute animal videos. *Famulus* (Pesopluma, 2020) is her debut book.

CONSTANCE RENFROW's fiction has appeared in such places as *Litro, Red Earth Review,* and *Mud Season Review*. Her short story "The Urg" won the Porter House Review Prize for Fiction and was selected for Best of the Net 2019. Her first book, *Songs of My Selfie,* an anthology of millennial fiction, was an IndieFAB finalist. She received her MFA in

Fiction from Pacific University, and she has recently completed her first novel. Visit her at constancerenfrow.com or follow her on Twitter @MissConstance21.

JOSEPHINE SLOYAN lives in Chicago. She has previously been published in *Room Magazine*.

GRACE Q. SONG is a writer residing in New York. Her poetry and fiction have been published or are forthcoming in *SmokeLong Quarterly*, *Passages North*, *PANK*, *The Journal*, *Zone 3*, and elsewhere. A high school senior, she plans to attend Columbia University in Fall 2021.

PRISCILLA THOMPSON works as a psychotherapist in New Hampshire, where she lives with her husband and three children. After taking a break from writing for nearly twenty years, she is surprised and grateful to *The South Carolina Review* for the opportunity to see her first short story in print.

ROBIN VIGFUSSON's stories have appeared in *Meat for Tea*, *Glassworks*, *Tower Journal*, *Constellations,* and other literary magazines. Her first collection of short stories was published in May 2021.

G.C. WALDREP's most recent books are *The Earliest Witnesses* (Tupelo/Carcanet, 2021) and *feast gently* (Tupelo, 2018), winner of the William Carlos Williams Award from the Poetry Society of America. Recent work has appeared or is forthcoming in *American Poetry Review*, *Poetry*, *Paris Review*, *New England Review*, *Yale Review*, *Colorado Review*, *The Nation*, *New American Writing*, *Conjunctions*, and other journals. Waldrep lives in Lewisburg, Pennsylvania, where he teaches at Bucknell University. In 2021 he is a Visiting Fellow at Clare Hall, Cambridge.

FRANCIS WALSH is a writer from coastal Maine, where they share an apartment with two rabbits and one human. Their work appears or is forthcoming in *Brevity*, the *Gateway Review*, and the *Los Angeles Review*. They can be reached on Instagram @walshfrancis.

ALEXANDRA PEER WATSON holds an MFA in fiction writing from Columbia, and a BA in English from Brown University. She is the co-founder and executive editor of *Apogee Journal*, a publication dedicated to highlighting marginalized voices, particularly writers and artists of color. Alexandra has taught in Columbia University's undergraduate writing program and at the nonprofit college access program Leadership Enterprise for a Diverse America, where she was the Assistant Director of Writing. Alexandra is currently a Lecturer in Barnard College's English Department and has had poetry and fiction published in *Lit Hub*, *[PANK]*, *Redivider*, *Nat. Brut.*, *Yes Poetry*, and *The Bennington Review*. She is the 2019 PEN/Nora Magid Prize for Literary Editing.

ERIN WILSON's poems have recently appeared or are forthcoming in *Salamander Magazine*, *Crab Creek Review*, *Reliquiae*, *Columba*, *Trinity House Review*, *Berfois*, *Pembroke Magazine*, *Hamilton Stone Review*, and in numerous other publications internationally. Her first collection is *At Home with Disquiet*, published by Circling Rivers Press. She lives and writes in a small town in northern Ontario, Canada.

JODY WINER's poems have appeared in *Epoch*, *The Massachusetts Review*, *Open City*, *phoebe*, *Poet Lore*, *The Saint Ann's Review*, and elsewhere. Her chapbook *Welcome to Guardian Angel School* won the 2019 Finishing Line Press Competition. A fellow of MacDowell and a Pushcart Prize nominee, she has worked as a librarian, writer, and dog wrangler.

KELSEY CARMODY WORT is an MFA candidate at Purdue University. She loves her home state of Wisconsin, her friends, and dancing around her kitchen.

ALICE YANG lives in St. Louis, but her heart belongs to Albuquerque. She's barely hanging onto the corporate ladder, dead-eyed, but it's kind of exciting sometimes. She finds laughter in her own trauma, has not been published previously, and appreciates butter more than anyone. She's a Kraken-believer and is convinced Nessie was a plesiosaur.

CPSIA information can be obtained
at www.ICGtesting.com
Printed in the USA
LVHW020432051121
702486LV00005B/14